A Guide To Common Sense Macroeconomics

Dr. Susan Dadres

Liberty Press
Richardson, Texas
Email: liberty@libertyidea.com

Published by Liberty Press

ISBN: 0939352-89-3

Table of Contents

Preface

Preface

This book is a complement to Ravi Batra's *Common Sense Macroeconomics*. It is a study guide, and contains overviews, questions and answers to the material in various chapters of the original book. The guide should prove invaluable to a student, who wants to test his or her understanding of the original text.

A partial answer key is provided at the end of each chapter, that is to say, some questions are left unanswered, except in the smallish Chapter 1. This has been done for two reasons. First, the student should read the textbook thoroughly and avoid the easy way out of just studying these questions and quickly look at the answers. The guide cannot provide a complete understanding of macroeconomics; it is, after all, a supplement, not a substitute for the textbook. Second, the unanswered questions offer an option to instructors to use the guide to assign homework to their students. This way the teacher can test the students' knowledge of macroeconomics before giving them an exam.

Most chapters of the original text are comprehensible at the principles level. However, chapter 9 and possibly parts of chapter 14 are too advanced for the first-year student, and may be explored only if time permits.

Chapter 1: Microeconomic Foundations and Common Sense

Key Concepts

Macroeconomics is a study of the economic behavior of society. It differs from **microeconomics,** which is a study of the economic behavior of the individuals, families and firms that constitute society.

Microeconomic Foundations are the microeconomic theories regarding the behavior of individuals, families and firms. These theories are in turn used in explaining the macroeconomic behavior of society.

Neo-Keynesian Theory is the body of ideas that modifies the original ideas offered by an economist named John Maynard Keynes, who wrote his masterpiece, *The General Theory of Employment, Interest and Money*, in 1936.

A dogma is a theory that misleads people. It is deceptively appealing, but serves the interests of special interest groups and a small minority of influential individuals. A clear-cut example of a dogma is the idea that smoking enhances your vigor and beauty by helping you relax and forget your worries.

Econometrics is the study of testing hypotheses by combining economics and statistics. It uses complicated formulas and models to decide disputed theories.

Regressive Taxes are those that disproportionately burden the poor by making them pay a larger percentage of their incomes in taxes than the rich. The sales tax and the Social Security tax are prime examples.

The Phillips Curve represents a short run tradeoff between the rates of inflation and unemployment.

Chapter Overview

Since economics deals with human nature, economic theories should be based purely on common sense, which suggests that only one or two explanations of observed phenomena should suffice. A lot of popular ideas seem to flout generally accepted notions of rationality; they are simply dogmas that are untruthful and have no historical legs to stand upon.

Why should we make a distinction between common sense and dogmas? History reveals time and again that dogmas can devastate an economy. Today we believe that the Great Depression, which plagued the world for ten long years in the 1930s, was mostly caused by faulty government policies

But we forget that what encouraged these policies were the dogmas of contemporary economists. Similarly, during the 1970s the world suffered from what may be called the Great Inflation. Here again economic policy, and another dogma of the day, turned a mild jump in prices into a persistent and enduring escalation.

The most popular dogma today is that low income tax rates, but not other types of taxes, offer an incentive to save, work hard, and invest, and thus stimulate economic growth. Yet history thoroughly contradicts the low-income-tax theology. All you need to explore its validity is one readily available fact: *During the 1950s and the 60s, economic growth was much stronger than in the 1970s, 80s and 90s even though the marginal income tax rate on top earning families, at less than 39 percent today, was as high as 91 percent in the past.*

Common sense propositions find ready support from observed facts, but dogmas need the crutch of sophistry, statistical techniques and econometrics. Although the low-income tax doctrine sounds self-serving and seems designed to further the interest of those paying high income taxes, it is the cornerstone of economic policy today, and is clearly not working. For the first time since the Great Depression, employment has declined for three straight years.

Thus we need to study macroeconomic theories with a critical eye, using the litmus test of common sense, which in turn is readily supported by unmanipulated facts of history.

True-False Questions: Indicate whether the following statements are (T)rue or (F)alse:

_____ 1.   Economists have proven conclusively that lowering income tax rates will improve incentives to work, save, and invest, resulting in more rapid economic growth and improved living standards.

_____ 2.   A tax is regressive when the tax rate falls as income rises and progressive when the tax rate rises as income rises.

_____ 3.   When income tax rates were very high in the 1950s and 1960s, economic growth was very strong by historical standards.

_____ 4.   During the 1990s, a rising income tax rate caused GDP growth to stagnate below the level in the 1980s.

_____ 5.   Today, many economists believe that the Great Depression was primarily the result of poor government policies.

_____ 6.   Advocates of a _laissez-faire_ approach to government policy usually believe that the economy will function more efficiently with a minimal amount of government intervention.

_____ 7.   The Phillips Curve model is based on the assumption that there exists a short- run tradeoff between inflation and unemployment, indicating that the unemployment rate can be reduced by permitting a higher rate of inflation.

_____ 8.   Real wages have steadily risen for a majority of workers since 1972, causing living standards to rise even as the average number of hours worked per week by the typical family has declined.

_____ 9.   Globalization unambiguously benefits everyone in a nation without harming any.

_____ 10.   Since the 1970s, income inequality and the concentration of wealth have been rising in the U.S. economy as well as in many other countries.

Discussion Questions

1.   Explain the meaning of the phrase "microeconomic foundation".

2.   Use a specific historical example to illustrate why <u>dogmas</u> can be dangerous for the economy.

3.   Explain what is meant by the phrase in the text "efficiency and ethics go together."

The Answer Key

True/False: 1. F 2. T 3. T 4. F 5. T 6. T 7. T 8. F 9. F 10. T

Discussion: 1. See page 1of the textbook; 2. See page 7; 3. See page 10

Chapter 2: The General Standard of Living

The goal of Macroeconomics is
To raise the living standard of all
To erase poverty and unemployment
For people big and small

These four lines aptly describe what macroeconomics is all about. It's about raising the general standard of living.

Key Concepts

"**Real**," in economics, means purchasing power.

The general standard of living in a country is popularly described by the purchasing power of its gross domestic product (GDP), which is a monetary yardstick of a country's total output during a year. It is also known as **real GDP**

Real per-capita GDP equals real GDP divided by the nation's population.

The distribution of GDP is just as important in determining the living standard. If the distribution among individuals becomes more and more unequal over time, real GDP and real per-capita GDP become misleading measures of the living standard.

The Average Real Wage is the purchasing power of the nation's overall wage rate divided by employed workers. This is a better measure of the living standard than GDP and per-capita GDP.

The Real Production Wage is the average real wage of production or non-supervisory workers, who constitute as much as 80% of the workforce. This is the best measure of the living standard in the United States, because it applies to the vast majority of people.

Fringe benefits are non-cash payments that workers receive from their employers. They include health insurance and pensions.

A CEO (chief executive officer) is the head a company but answerable to the firm's board of governors.

Wage gap may be defined by national labor productivity divided by the national real wage.

CPI (consumer price index) is an average price of goods commonly consumed by society.

Inflation occurs when prices rise systematically.

Deflation occurs when prices fall systematically.

A tax haven is a country where taxes are much lower than those in other countries.

A tariff is a tax on imports.

Globalization refers to increasing linkage to the world's economies by means of international trade and investment.

A closed economy (or autarky) is one where foreign trade is zero or extremely low.

An open economy is one where foreign trade is a large percentage of GDP.

A trade deficit occurs when exports fall short of imports. A *trade surplus* means a negative trade deficit.

Chapter Overview

The real production wage is the best measure of the living standard in the United States. From 1800 to 1972, the production wage, along with other measures of the living standard, rose every decade. But since 1972, the real wage of the non-supervisory worker has been falling while other measures continue to rise. *Thus, the vast majority of Americans, over three-fourths of the labor force, has seen a drop in their living standard ever since 1972.* A large portion of per-capita GDP growth has gone to the group of CEOs, who, in 2002, earned an average wage that was 510 times the production wage.

The general standard of living is also determined by the unemployment rate, which has generally declined after WWII. Prices of goods and services play a crucial role in the living standard. Until 1940 they went up as well as down in the United States, but have been on an upward march ever since. Another important factor is the structure and size of taxation. Until 1913, the primary source of government revenue were tariffs, which were gradually replaced by the individual income tax to pave the way for free trade.

Another levy, the Social-Security tax, was introduced in 1935, and by now it is the second largest source of revenue. With the fall in tariffs has come the globalization of the American economy, where the service sector reigns supreme, employing as much as 75 percent of the labor force. Manufacturing, anther other important sector, grew sharply in the 19th and the early part of the 20th century, but employed only 12 percent of labor in 2003. This is not much above the employment-share of manufacturing in 1800, when the share stood at just 5%. Since 1980 the trade deficit has zoomed, turning the United States into the largest debtor in the world.

True-False Questions

Indicate whether the following statements are (T)rue or (F)alse:

_____ 1.   An increase in real per-capita GDP indicates that the economy's total output is increasing faster than the growth in population.

_____ 2.   In a growing economy, output always becomes more equally distributed to ensure that living standards are rising.

_____ 3.   Production workers, or those in non-supervisory jobs, comprise approximately 75 to 80 percent of the labor force.

_____ 4.   If Bill received an 8 percent increase in his nominal salary at the same time that prices rose on average by 5 percent, then his purchasing power increased by approximately 3 percent.

_____ 5.   In the 1960s, the compensation of chief executive officers (CEOs) was about 41 times as large as the production wage and this multiple has remained virtually unchanged since then.

_____ 6.   The wage gap has increased in the past 40 years, indicating that real wages are rising much faster than worker productivity is improving.

_____ 7.   The rate of unemployment in the U.S. economy has been relatively low since peaking at close to 25 percent in 1933.

_____ 8.   Since 1940, the consumer price index (CPI) has steadily increased, implying that deflation is a thing of the past.

_____ 9.   In 1913, the 16th amendment to the U.S. Constitution paved the way for an income tax on individuals and corporations, permitting much less reliance on tariffs as a means of raising government revenue.

_____ 10.   Since the 1980s, U.S. exports have increased more rapidly than imports, resulting in substantial trade surpluses.

Multiple Choice – circle the best response:

1.   The most well known measure for the standard of living in a country is the:
      a. rate at which its economy is growing.
      b. size of its population.
      c. purchasing power of its gross domestic product (GDP).
      d. nominal size of its gross domestic product (GDP).

2.   To account for both population growth and inflation, it is useful to gauge living standards using the:

a. average number of hours worked per week.

b. nominal earnings per worker.

c. nominal per-capita GDP.

d. real per-capita GDP.

3.   A rise in both real GDP and real per-capita GDP:

a.   may not correspond to an increase in everyone's living standards if output is unequally distributed.

b.   may not correspond to an increase in everyone's living standards if output is equally distributed.

c. necessarily means that each individual is experiencing a higher living standard.

d. necessarily means that most individuals are experiencing a lower living standard, while only the richest are experiencing a higher living standard.

4.   The production wage is the:

a. average real wage of non-supervisory workers.

b. average nominal wage of non-supervisory workers.

c. average real wage of supervisory workers.

d. average nominal wage of supervisory workers.

5.   Since 1972 in the U.S.:

a. real per-capita GDP has declined.

b. the average real wage has risen.

c. the production wage has declined.

d. all of the above have occurred.

6.   Which of the following has risen the most significantly in the U.S. since 1972?

a. The minimum wage mandated by government

b. The average compensation of corporate chief executive officers (CEOs)

c. The production wage

d. The average real wage of non-supervisory workers

7.   The wage gap is a measure of:
        a. the average compensation of chief executive officers (CEOs).
        b. the average real earning of non-supervisory workers.
        c. the real wage divided by labor productivity.
        d. labor productivity divided by the real wage.

8.   If, over time, the wage gap is constant, then:
        a. the real wage is growing faster than labor productivity.
        b. the real wage is growing at the same rate as labor productivity.
        c. the real wage is growing slower than labor productivity.
        d. neither the real wage nor labor productivity are changing.

9.   When U.S. policymakers sought to promote international trade by reducing import tariffs in the early 20th century, federal government revenues were generated by:
        a. selling government assets.
        b. borrowing.
        c. taxing the incomes of individuals and corporations.
        d. taxing consumption using a national sales tax.

10.   The relative importance of agriculture in the U.S. economy has:
        a. fallen significantly while the relative importance of the service sector has grown.
        b. grown significantly while the relative importance of the service sector has fallen.
        c. not changed, but the relative importance of the service sector has grown.
        c. fallen, but the relative importance of the service sector has not changed.

Problems and Discussion Questions:

1.   Define and explain the significance of a) GDP, b) real GDP, and c) real per-capita GDP.

2.   Mary's salary increased from $36,000 last year to $38,000 this year. If the
        economy experienced 4 percent inflation over the last year, has Mary's purchasing power
                increased along with her salary? Calculate the real value of Mary's current salary
                in terms of last year's prices.

3.   Define the production wage and explain why the behavior of the average real wage
        might differ from the behavior of the production wage over time. What sort of
        trend has the production wage followed since 1972? How do you interpret this in
        terms of the living standards of production workers?

4 .   What specific social trends might be used to confirm a reduced living standard in
        The U.S. since 1972?

5.   Explain what has happened to CEO Pay (the compensation paid to chief executive officers of U.S. corporations) compared to the production wage since 1960. Does CEO pay appear to be sensitive to the state of the economy?

Define the wage gap and describe how this measure has changed since 1972. If You became twice as productive at your job, would you expect to be paid twice as much? What do you think causes workers to become more productive?

7.   What was the main purpose of the 16th amendment to the U.S. Constitution? After introducing an income tax with low rates, why did policymakers increase the income tax rates so drastically?

8.   Describe how the allocation of resources among the major sectors of the economy (farming, services, and manufacturing) has changed in U.S. history.

The Answer Key

True/False: 1. T   2. F   3. T   4. T   5. F   6. F   7. T   8. T   9. T   10. F

Multiple Choice: 1. C;   2. D;   3. A;   4. A;   5. C;   6. B;   7. D;   8. B;   9. C;   10. A

Problems/Discussion: 1. See pages 12-13 of the textbook; 2. Mary's salary rose approximately 5½% while inflation was 4%, so her purchasing power increased. Mary's current real income = $38,000/1.04 = $36,538, which is slightly higher than her base salary of $36,000.
3. See page 14 4. See pages 17-18 ; 5. See pages 18-19; 6. See pages 20-21; 7. See pages 26-28; 8. See pages 31-33

Chapter 3: GDP Accounting

Key Concepts

GDP or gross domestic product is the retail value of all final goods and services produced in a country during a year.

Intermediate goods are goods that are used up in the production of other goods within a year. Copper, seeds, aluminum, plastics, etc. are prime examples of such goods

Capital goods are goods that are also used up in the production of other goods but last longer than a year. Machines, roads, bridges, parks and office buildings, etc. are thus capital or **investment goods.**

Consumption goods are all other goods. They are utilized by society to satisfy the day-to-day needs.

$$\textbf{NDP} = \text{GDP} - \text{Capital Consumption}$$

Here capital consumption is the depreciation that capital goods suffer every year, and are actually a cost not production for society, and NDP is net domestic product.

$$\textbf{Domestic income} = \text{NDP} - \text{indirect business taxes}$$

Indirect taxes include the sales tax and the excise tax.

$$\textbf{National income} = \text{domestic income} + \text{NFP}$$

Here NFP is net factor payment from abroad, and equals the difference between income earned from abroad and that paid to those in foreign countries.

$$\textbf{GNP} = \text{GDP} + \text{NFP}$$

Here GNP stands for gross national product.

$$\textbf{Personal income} = \text{national income} - \text{corporate retention} + \text{transfer payments} + \text{government interest}$$

where

$$\text{corporate retention} = \text{corporate taxes} + \text{payroll taxes} + \text{retained earnings.}$$

Personal disposable income = personal income − personal taxes

Chapter Overview

There are three approaches to measuring GDP.

      a. The expenditure approach

      b. The income approach

and

      c. The value-added approach

In the expenditure approach,

$$GDP = C + I + G + X - M$$

In the income approach,

$$GDP = \text{national income} + \text{capital consumption} + \text{indirect taxes}$$

where

$$\text{National income} = \text{Wages} + \text{Interest} + \text{Rent} + \text{Profit} + \text{Proprietor's Income}$$

In the value added approach,

$$GDP = \text{Sum of the value added of all firms}$$

where

$$\text{Value added of a firm} = \text{a firm's total revenue} - \text{payments to other firms for intermediate goods}$$

Other Important Formulas

When nominal values are adjusted for changes in prices, we obtain real values. Thus,

$$\text{Real GDP} = \text{Nominal GDP/price level}$$

and

$$\text{Price level} = \text{a price index} / 100$$

The price index used to obtain real GDP from its nominal value is called the GDP deflator, or simply the deflator.

$$\text{GDP deflator} = (\text{Nominal GDP} \div \text{real GDP}) \times 100$$

$$= \frac{[\underline{\text{value of current output at current prices}}]}{\text{value of current output at base year prices}} \times 100.$$

The deflator is thus nominal GDP expressed as a percentage of real GDP. Similarly

$$\text{Real GDP} = (\text{nominal GDP/the deflator}) \times 100.$$

$$\text{Inflation rate} = (\text{change in the deflator} \div \text{the previous year's deflator}) \times 100$$

Or

$$\text{Inflation rate} = (\text{change in the CPI} \div \text{the previous year's CPI}) \times 100$$

$$\text{GDP Growth Rate in 2003} = \left(\frac{\underline{\text{Increase in Real GDP in 2003}}}{\text{Real GDP in 2002}} \right) \times 100$$

Other Important Concepts

The purchasing power of any monetary variable relative to the prices of a base year is called its real value. A monetary measure is called a nominal variable, one that is obtained by using current prices. If prices are constant then real and nominal values are the same.

When nominal values are adjusted for changes in prices, we get real values. Real GDP is current output valued at some base year's prices. The real wage is defined by nominal wage as a percentage of the consumer price index (CPI), which is the nominal value of a market basket of commonly used goods and services expressed as a percentage of their real value.

The rate of inflation is the change in a price index expressed as a percentage of the previous year's price. Negative inflation is deflation.

U.S. history reveals that in normal circumstances inflation has peaked every third decade. So has money growth. Thus the cycle of inflation runs parallel to the cycle of money growth, indicating that high money growth breeds inflation. Both the cycles have an impeccable forecasting record. They now suggest that the first decade of the 21st century is likely to be inflationary.

U.S. history also reveals that real GDP growth follows a cyclical path, both in the short run and in the long run. This creates a growth cycle. A special case of the growth cycle is called the business cycle, in which GDP growth is positive as well as negative. A business cycle normally has five phases that include a recession, trough, expansion, boom and a peak. A recession is said to occur when real GDP declines consecutively over two quarters, and normally generates negative or zero growth for the year.

Inflation generally hurts the money lender and the weakest sections of society such as the minimum-wage earners, the retirees and older workers, and generally benefits the borrower as the strongest social groups.

3.1 True-False Questions

Circle T for true and F for false.

T   F   1.   According to the cycle of inflation, the 1830s were a peak decade of inflation even though the actual inflation rate during the decade was close to zero.

T   F   2.   A fall in the price of missiles will cause the GDP deflator to fall if no other price changes, while the CPI is unchanged.

T   F   3.   Both capital and intermediate goods are used up in the production process.

T   F   4.   Domestic Income = GDP -   direct business taxes - depreciation.

T   F   5.   Personal disposable income = Personal Income - all taxes.

T   F   6.   Transfer payments include government payments for social security and welfare.

T   F   7.   If you add the production value of all firms in an economy in a year, you get GDP for that year.

T   F   8.   In the GDP accounting system, $GDP = C + I + G + M - X$.

T   F   9.   If NFP is small, domestic income is close to national income.

T   F   10.   If the trade deficit is zero, then domestic spending equals GDP.

3.2 Multiple Choice Questions: Circle the best answer.

1.   If nominal GDP increases:
   a.   real GDP must also have increased.
   b.   prices must also have increased.
   c.   real GDP may have increased or decreased.
   d.   employment must have increased.

2.	If nominal GDP in the current period is $600 billion, the CPI is 200 and the GDP deflator is 300, then real GDP is equal to:
   a.	$300 billion.
   b.	$200 billion.
   c.	$600 billion.
   d.	$100billion.

3.	National income can be calculated as
   a.	GDP - depreciation - indirect business taxes + NFP
   b.	as payments to all factors of production
   c.	by adding wages, interest, rents, proprietor's incomes and profits
   d.	all of the above.

4.	Which of the following is an intermediate good?
   a.	A car purchased by an individual.
   b.	A car purchased by a taxi cab company.
   c.	A car purchased by the federal government.
   d.	Gasoline purchased by an individual.
   e.	Gasoline purchased by a taxi cab company.

5.	An accumulation of unsold goods is
   a.	counted in GDP as investment.
   b.	counted in GDP as consumption.
   c.	counted in GDP, but not as consumption or investment.
   d.	not counted in GDP.

6.	According to the cycle of inflation, the inflation peaks occurred in the
   a.	1860s
   b.	1770s
   c.	1970s
   d.	all of the above.

7. According to the Cycle of Money Growth, money growth peaked during the
   a.	1860s
   b.	1770s
   c.	1970s
   d.	1910s
   e.	all of the above.

8. Inflation hurts
    a. the weakest sections of society
    b. the money lender
    c. the minimum-wage earner
    d. all of the above.

9. When does an intermediate good become a final good?
    a. never
    b. whenever it is used for consumption by an individual
    c. when some raw materials remain unsold at the end of the year
    d. both "b" and "c."

10. Net Domestic Product (NDP) is defined as:
    a. GDP + Depreciation
    b. GDP - Depreciation
    c. GDP - capital consumption
    d. Both b and c.

3.3   **Indicate whether the following statements are** (T)rue or (F)alse:

_____ 1.   Gross domestic product is the retail value of all final goods and services produced in a country during a year.

_____ 2.   The value of intermediate goods are counted more than once when a country's gross domestic product is estimated.

_____ 3.   GDP includes only new products, because goods produced in previous years were included in GDPs of the past.

_____ 4.   Net Domestic Product deducts from GDP the wear and tear that capital goods undergo in the production process.

_____ 5.   Domestic Income is always exactly equal to National Income.

_____ 6.   GDP usually determines a country's employment, whereas GNP generates its living standard.

_____ 7.   If exports exceed imports, then net exports are positive and a country has a trade deficit.

_____ 8.   National income represents the total amount of income that people have available to either spend or save.

_____ 9. After subtracting corporate retention, transfer payments and government interest are added to National Income to arrive at Personal Income.

_____ 10. The sum of consumption expenditure and household saving equals Personal Disposable Income.

3.4 **Multiple Choice – circle the best answer:**

1. Gross Domestic Product can best be defined as the:
   a. retail value of all final goods and services produced in a country during a year.
   b. wholesale value of all final goods and services produced in a country during a year.
   c. retail value of all intermediate goods and services produced in a country during a year.
   d. wholesale value of all intermediate goods and services produced in a country during a year.

2. Which of the following are examples of intermediate, rather than final, goods?
   a. steel, cotton, aluminum, and plastics
   b. personal computers, copy machines, and fax machines
   c. machines, roads, bridges, parks, and office buildings
   d. food, clothing, and healthcare services

3. When an automobile manufacturer purchases steel and other raw materials for $250,000 and uses these materials to produce automobiles which are then sold for $800,000, the resulting increase in gross domestic product is:
   a. $1,050,000
   b. $250,000
   c. $550,000
   d. $800,000

4. Clara purchased $300,000 worth of clothing that was manufactured domestically during the year, but sold only $250,000 before the end of the year. As a result, we would count:
   a. $300,000 in consumption spending.
   b. $250,000 in consumption spending and $50,000 in investment spending.
   c. $300,000 in investment spending.
   d. $250,000 in consumption spending and $300,000 in investment spending.

5. Capital consumption, also called depreciation, is a measure of:
   a. the total amount of taxes paid by businesses that conduct capital investment.
   b. the difference between national income and personal income.
   c. the value of capital equipment that has been purchased during the year.
   d. the value of capital equipment that has been used up, worn out, or become obsolete.

6.   Net Domestic Product is equal to Gross Domestic Product:
        a. minus net factor payments from abroad.
        b. plus net factor payments from abroad.
        c. minus capital consumption.
        d. plus capital consumption.

7.   Gross National Product is equal to Gross Domestic Product:
        a. plus capital consumption.
        b. minus capital consumption.
        c. plus net factor payments from abroad.
        d. minus net factor payments from abroad.

8.   From the expenditure approach, Gross Domestic Product is equal to:
        a. C + I + G + X + M
        b. C + I + G + X - M
        c. C + I + G - X - M
        d. C + I + G

9.   If net exports are negative, then:
        a. imports exceed exports and the country has a trade deficit.
        b. imports exceed exports and the country has a trade surplus.
        c. exports exceed imports and the country has a trade deficit.
        d. exports exceed imports and the country has a trade surplus.

10.   If net exports are positive, then:
        a. imports exceed exports and the country has a trade deficit.
        b. imports exceed exports and the country has a trade surplus.
        c. exports exceed imports and the country has a trade deficit.
        d. exports exceed imports and the country has a trade surplus.

3.5   **Multiple Choice** – circle the best answer:

1.   Net National Product equals:
      a. Gross National Product – indirect taxes.
      b. Gross National Product + indirect taxes.
      c. National income + indirect taxes.
      d. National income – indirect taxes.

2.   Net National Product equals:
      a. Gross National Product – Capital Consumption.
      b. Gross National Product + Capital Consumption.
      c. National income – Capital Consumption.
      d. National income + Capital Consumption.

3.   Gross National Product equals:
      a. Gross Domestic Product – net factor payments from abroad.
      b. Gross Domestic Product + net factor payments from abroad.
      c. Gross Domestic Product – Capital Consumption.
      d. Gross Domestic Product + Capital Consumption.

Use the data below to answer questions 4 – 10:

Personal Consumption Expenditure	$7,300 billion
Gross Private Domestic Investment	$1,640 billion
Consumption of Fixed Capital (Depreciation)	$1,425 billion
Government Purchases of Goods and Services	$2,260 billion
Exports	$1,210 billion
Imports	$1,525 billion
Indirect Business Taxes	$665 billion
Net Factor Payments from abroad	- $25 billion

4.   Gross Domestic Product (GDP) is equal to:
a. $10,860 billion.
b. $10,885 billion.
c. $12,285 billion.
d. $12,310 billion.

5.   Net Domestic Product (NDP) is equal to:
a. $9,435 billion.
b. $9,445 billion.
c. $9,450 billion.
d. $9,460 billion

6.   Gross National Product (GNP) is equal to:
a. $10,860 billion.
b. $10,885 billion.
c. $12,285 billion.
e. $12,310 billion.

7.   Net National Product (NNP) is equal to:
a. $9,435 billion.
b. $9,445 billion.
c. $9,450 billion.
d. $9,460 billion.

8.   Domestic Income is equal to:
a. $8,770 billion.
b. $8,780 billion.
c. $8,795 billion.
e. $9,435 billion.

9. National Income is equal to:
    a. $8,770 billion.
    b. $8,780 billion.
    c. $8,795 billion.
    d. $9,435 billion.

10. Net exports are equal to:
    a. $2,735 billion.
    b. - $2,735 billion.
    c. $315 billion.
    d. - $315 billion.

3.6   Problems and Discussion Questions:

1. Use the data below to fill in the blanks and calculate GDP and GNP.

Personal Consumption Expenditure		_____
Durable Goods	840	
Nondurable Goods	2,000	
Services	4,200	
Gross Private Domestic Investment		_____
Business Fixed Investment	1,750	
Inventory Investment	-50	
Government Purchases of Goods and Services		1,850
Net Exports		-350
Exports	_____	
Imports	1,350	
Net Factor Payment	-20	

GDP (Gross Domestic Product) = _____

GNP (Gross National Product) = _____

2. Explain the difference between GDP (Gross Domestic Product) and GNP (Gross National Product).

3. Use the data to calculate National Income, Net National Product, Gross National Product, and Gross Domestic Product.

Compensation of Employees	5,950
Proprietor's Income	725
Rental Income of Persons	135
Corporate Profits	740
Net Interest	650
Indirect Business Taxes	655
Consumption of Fixed Capital	1,380
Factor Income Received from Rest of the World	320
Payments of Factor Income to Rest of the World	305

National Income = _____

Net National Product = _____

Gross National Product = _____

Gross Domestic Product = _____

4. What are the 3 ways to measure and estimate GDP? What is the relationship between Income, Output, and Expenditure for an economy?

3.7   **Indicate whether the following statements are (T)rue or (F)alse:**

_____ 1.   Real GDP is the value of the economy's production of all final goods using the constant prices of a base year.

_____ 2.   An increase in real GDP could mean that output is rising, or that prices are rising, or that both output and prices are rising.

_____ 3.   A new type of deflator called the chained price index uses average unit prices for any two consecutive years instead of a single base year.

_____ 4.   The CPI is computed by using the same method as the deflator, except that the market basket is fixed and includes only items commonly entering into people's consumption in the base year.

_____ 5.   The rate of inflation is calculated as the percentage change in a price index.

_____ 6.   The economy's growth rate is calculated as the percentage change in nominal GDP.

_____ 7.   The economy's rate of growth has been negative in as many years as it has been positive.

_____ 8.   The cycle of inflation, which is described by price growth per decade, follows an oscillating path throughout American history.

_____ 9.   In a growing economy, the money supply must increase to accommodate a larger number of transactions and keep the price level stable.

_____ 10.   If inflation is higher than anticipated, interest rates go up but long-term borrowers with a fixed rate of interest are not hurt by this.

3.8   **Multiple Choice – circle the best response:**

1.   If nominal GDP has doubled and the current price level is 2, then:
    a. real GDP has doubled as well.
    b. real GDP has increased, but has not doubled.
    c. real GDP has fallen.
    d. real GDP has not changed.

2.   If nominal GDP has doubled and the current price level is 1.5, then:
        a. real GDP has doubled as well.
        b. real GDP has increased, but has not doubled.
        c. real GDP has fallen.
        d. real GDP has not changed.

3.   Real GDP is best defined as:
        a. nominal GDP multiplied by the price level.
        b. the total production of goods, excluding the value of all services.
        c. the value of the economy's production of all final goods using the prices of the base
           year.
        d. the value of the economy's production of all final goods using the prices of the
           current year.

4.   If the Consumer Price index (CPI) in year 1 was 120 and 129.36 in year 2, then the rate of
        inflation between year 1 and year 2 was:
        a. 9.36 percent.
        b. 7.8 percent.
        c. 6.9 percent.
        d. 3.4 percent.

5.   If a worker's nominal wage rate increases from $5 to $6 while the price index increases
        from 100 to 125, then:
        a. the worker's real wage rate has fallen.
        b. the increase in nominal wages is not high enough to cover inflation.
        c. the worker will have less purchasing power.
        d. all of the above are true.

6.   In year 1 the CPI is 100, and in year 2 the CPI is 106.5. If Sarah's salary was $32,500 in
        year 1, what salary in year 2 would keep the real value of her salary the same as in year
        1?
        a. $41,535.00.
        b. $30,516.50
        c. $39,000.00.
        d. $34,612.50.

7.   Sally heard on the news that the rate of inflation is 2.7 percent and she was just informed that her salary is being raised 7 percent. Based on this information, which of the following is true?
        a. Sally's real income is increasing 4.3 percent.
        b. Sally's real income is decreasing 4.3 percent.
        c. Sally's nominal income is increasing 9.7 percent.
        d. Sally's nominal income is decreasing 9.7 percent.

8.   The five phases of the typical business cycle, in order of appearance, are:
        a. peak, trough, boom, recession, expansion.
        b. expansion, boom, recession, trough, peak.
        c. recession, trough, expansion, boom, peak.
        d. recession, boom, trough, peak, expansion.

9.   Over the past 250 years, the decennial rate of inflation has:
        a. reached a peak every other decade.
        b. reached a peak every third decade and then usually declined over the next two.
        c. gradually increased, reaching a new peak in each consecutive decade.
        d. followed a pattern that is completely different from the decennial rate of money growth.

10.   Which of the following is *least* likely to be hurt by inflation?
        a. borrowers, when inflation is unanticipated.
        b. unskilled workers earning the minimum wage.
        c. retirees on a fixed income.
        d. lenders, when inflation is unanticipated.

3.9   Problems:

1.   Use the hypothetical data below to answer the questions.

	Apples		Oranges	
	Price	Quantity	Price	Quantity
Year 1 (Base)	$1	20	$2	10
Year 2 (Current)	$1.50	15	$2.20	15

Assume the market basket used for the CPI includes 20 apples and 10 oranges. If the base value of the CPI is 100, what is the current value of the CPI? What is the rate of inflation between year 1 and year 2 according to the CPI?

        Current CPI = _____   Inflation Rate = _____

2.   Fill in the blanks:

Year	Nominal GDP	Real GDP	GDP Deflator
1	_____	$7,200 billion	100
2	$8,118 billion	_____	110
3	$8,750 billion	$7,675.2 billion	_____

The economy's growth rate is _____% from year 1 to year 2 and _____% from year 2 to year 3.

3.   Use the hypothetical data below to answer the questions.

	Apples		Oranges	
	Price	Quantity	Price	Quantity
Year 1 (Base)	$1	10	$2	10
Year 2 (Current)	$1.50	10	$2.10	20

Assume the market basket used for the CPI includes 10 apples and 10 oranges. If the base value of the CPI is 100, what is the current value of the CPI? What is the rate of inflation between year 1 and year 2 according to the CPI?

        Current CPI = _____   Inflation Rate = _____

4.   Fill in the blanks:

Year	Nominal GDP	Real GDP	GDP Deflator
1	_____	$7,800 billion	100
2	$8,435.7 billion	_____	105
3	$9,240 billion	$8,400 billion	_____

The economy's growth rate is _____% from year 1 to year 2 and _____% from year 2 to year 3.

3.10 More Numerical Problems

1. Examine the following table

Output in 2004	Unit Price in 2004	Unit Price in the Base Year (1996)
20 tons of food	$14	$4
100 houses	22	6
120 machines	6	5
80 pairs of shoes	5	$6.50
40 tons of copper	3	2

Using various definitions, calculate the following for the year 2004

a. nominal GDP

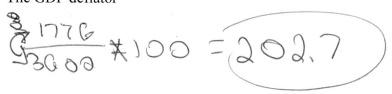

$14 \times 20 +$
$22 \times 100 +$
$6 \times 120 +$
$5 \times 80 =$

$280 + 2,200 + 720 + 2100$ $\$3,600$

b. real GDP

4×20
6×100
5×120
$6.5 \times 80 =$

$80 + 600 + 600 + 496$ $\$1776$

c. The GDP deflator

$\dfrac{1776}{3600} \times 100 = 202.7$

d. Business investment for equipment, both nominal and real, assuming all capital goods were sold.

$6 \times 120 = \$720$ Nominal

$5 \times 120 = \$600$ real

e. Residential investment, both nominal and real, assuming all new homes were sold

$22 \times 100 = \$2200$ (nominal) $6 \times 100 = \$600$ (real)

f. Total investment (nominal and real) assuming that all machines and homes were sold during 2004, but 10 pairs of shoes and 8 tons of copper were not.

$((10 \times 5) + (8 \times 3)) + (22 \times 100) + (6 \times 120) = \$2994$ (nominal) $74 + 2200 + 720$

$((10 \times 6.5) + (8 \times 2)) + (6 \times 100) + (5 \times 120) = \$1281$ (real) $81 + 600 + 600$

g. nominal and real consumption, assuming that the production of all consumption goods was the same in 2004 and the base year.

$(20 \times 14) + (80 \times 5) = \$680$ (nominal)   food, shoes

$(20 \times 4) + (80 \times 6.5) = \$600$ (real)   food, shoes

h. The CPI

2. Examine the following figures:

C = 1500, I = 500, G = 600, X = 700, M = 800, depreciation = 200, indirect taxes = 300, NFP = 0, corporate retention = 500, transfer payments = 400, government interest = 200, personal or direct taxes = 500.

Calculate the following:

a.   GDP

b.   NDP

c.   National Income

d.   Personal Income

e.   Personal disposable income

f. Personal or household savings

3. Examine the following figures:

Wages = 100, rent = 10, interest income = 20, profit = 30, proprietor's income = 5, government's interest payment = 15, transfer payment = 50, capital consumption = 10, indirect taxes = 5, direct taxes = 18. Calculate, if NFP=0

a. national income

b. NDP

c. GDP

The Answer Key

True-False Questions:

3.1:   Find your answers

3.2   Multiple choice: 1.C; 2. B; 3. D; 4. E; 5. A; 6. D; 7. E; 8. D; 9. D; 10. D

3.3   True/False: Find your answers

3.4   Multiple Choice: 1. A 2. A 3. D 4. B 5. D 6. C 7. C 8. B 9. A 10. D

3.5 Multiple Choice: 1. C 2. A 3. B 4. B 5. D 6. A 7. A 8. C 9. A 10. D

3.6   Problems/Discussion:
   1. Personal Consumption Expenditure = 7,040; Gross Private
   Domestic Investment = 1,700; Exports = 1,000; GDP = 10,240; GNP = 10,220.
   2. GDP measures the economic activity that takes place within a country whereas GNP
   measures the economic activity of a country's nationals; GNP = GDP + NFP, where
   NFP is net factor payments from abroad.
   3. National Income = 8,200; Net National Product = 8,855; Gross National Product =
   10,235; Gross Domestic Product = 10,220. 4. The 2 ways are the expenditure approach,
   the income approach, and the value-added approach; Income = Output = Expenditure.

3.7   True/False: 1. T 2. F 3. T 4. T 5. T 6. F 7. F 8. T 9. T 10. T

3.8   Multiple Choice: 1. D 2. B 3. C. 4. B 5. D 6. D 7. A 8. C 9. B 10. A

3.9   Problems:
   1. CPI = 130; inflation rate = 30%.
   2. Nominal GDP = 7,200 billion in year 1; real GDP = 7,380 in year 2; GDP Deflator = 114
   in year 3; growth rate = 2.5% from year 1 to year 2 and 4% from year 2 to year 3.
   3. CPI = 120; inflation rate = 20%.
   4. Nominal GDP = 7,800 billion in year 1; real GDP = 8,034 in year 2; GDP Deflator = 110
   in year 3; growth rate = 3% from year 1 to year 2 and 4.5% from year 2 to year 3.

3.10 Numerical Problems: Find your answers

CHAPTER 4: THE CLASSICAL MICRO MODEL

Key Concepts

The Invisible Hand is an idea pioneered by Adam Smith. It refers to the self interest of consumers and producers that motivates them to interact with each other, generating an efficient and productive economic system.

Demand and Supply: Smith's invisible hand is today described by the concepts of supply and demand.

The Law of Demand is that, other things remaining the same, a person buys more of a product as its price falls, and less of a product as its price rises.

The Law of supply is that, other things remaining the same, a firm produces more of a product as its price rises and less of the product as its price falls.

Equilibrium refers to a state in which those interacting in a market are satisfied with the outcome. It is a state of rest, where there is no pressure for change.

Equilibrium is a central concept in economics, because in normal times actual and equilibrium values are close to each other.

Market equilibrium occurs when supply equals demand in a market.

Chapter Overview

Supply and demand are like two prongs of a pair of scissors that defines the behavior of any industry or market. The demand curve has a negative slope representing a negative relationship between consumer purchases and the product price, whereas the supply curve has a positive slope that portrays a positive link between the product price and the production of that good. When both variables represented by a curve change simultaneously, the human behavior is represented by a **movement along that curve**. However, a change in only one of the two variables is represented by **a shift of the entire curve**, up or down.

Demand and supply describe classical microeconomics that also underlie classical macroeconomics.

True-False Questions

4.1   Indicate whether the following statements are (T)rue or (F)alse:

_____ 1.   The mechanism that brings the best out of producers and workers in Adam Smith's model is called the invisible hand of a free market.

_____ 2.   The pursuit of self-interest by everyone ensures that society's resources are put to their best use, even when markets are not competitive.

_____ 3.   The evolution of the American economy provides strong evidence in favor of Adam Smith's belief in the strength of the invisible hand.

_____ 4.   Other things remaining constant, an increase in the price of peanuts causes the quantity demanded of peanuts to fall.

_____ 5.   Other things remaining constant, an increase in the price of peanuts causes the quantity supplied of peanuts to fall.

_____ 6.   An increase in the price of Nike shirts would be expected to increase the demand for Polo shirts.

_____ 7.   If consumers decide to buy more clothing because of an increase in their incomes, the demand curve for clothing would shift rightward.

_____ 8.   If consumers decide to buy more clothing because of a decrease in the price of clothing, the demand curve for clothing would shift rightward.

_____ 9.   If firms decide to produce more clothing because the price of clothing has risen, the supply curve of clothing would shift rightward.

_____ 10.   If the quantity demanded and the quantity supplied are equal at a price of $5.00, then the equilibrium price is $5.00.

 4.2   **Multiple Choice** – circle the best response:

1.   According to the law of demand, other things remaining constant, an increase in price causes:
a. a decrease in quantity purchased.
b. an increase in quantity purchased.
c. a decrease in demand for related goods.
d. an increase in demand for related goods.

2.   According to the law of supply, other things remaining constant, an increase in price causes:
a. an increase in output.
b. a decrease in output.
c. an increase in supply of related goods.
d. a decrease in supply of related goods.

3.   Which of the following would best explain an increase in (or rightward shift of) demand?
a. an increase in the price of the item.
b. an increase in the cost of producing the item.
c. an increase in the price of a substitute item.
d. a decrease in the price of the item.

4.   Which of the following would best explain a decrease in (or leftward shift of) demand?
a. a decrease in the cost of producing the item.
b. a decrease in consumers' income.
c. an increase in the price of the item.
d. an increase in the price of a substitute item.

5.   Which of the following would best explain an increase in (or rightward shift of) supply?
a. a decrease in consumers' income.
b. an increase in the price of the item.
c. an increase in the cost of producing the item.
d. a reduction in the cost of producing the item.

6.   Which of the following would best explain a decrease in (or leftward shift of) supply?
a. an increase in consumers' income.
b. a decrease in the price of the item.
c. an increase in the cost of producing the item.
d. a reduction in the cost of producing the item.

7.   Equilibrium in a free market occurs where:
     a. supply and demand intersect.
     b. sellers in the market earn the maximum possible revenue.
     c. consumers in the market enjoy the maximum possible level of satisfaction.
     d. the amount of excess demand is exactly equal to the amount of excess supply.

8.   Other things remaining the same, especially favorable weather conditions would be expected to:
     a. increase the supply of tomatoes and raise the equilibrium price of tomatoes.
     b. decrease the supply of tomatoes and lower the equilibrium price of tomatoes.
     c. increase the supply of tomatoes and lower the equilibrium price of tomatoes.
     d. decrease the supply of tomatoes and raise the equilibrium price of tomatoes.

9.   Other things remaining the same, a decrease in the price of chicken (a substitute for beef) would be expected to:
     a. increase the demand for beef and lower the equilibrium price of beef.
     b. decrease the demand for beef and raise the equilibrium price of beef.
     c. increase the demand for beef and raise the equilibrium price of beef.
     d. decrease the demand for beef and lower the equilibrium price of beef.

10. Other things remaining the same, if the supply of widgets increases at the same time as the demand for widgets, then:
     a. the equilibrium quantity would increase with no change in equilibrium price.
     b. both the equilibrium price and quantity would increase.
     c. the equilibrium price would fall and the equilibrium quantity would increase.
     d. equilibrium quantity would increase, but the effect on equilibrium price cannot be known without additional information.

4.3   **Multiple Choice** – circle the best response:

Use the graph below to answer questions 1 – 3:

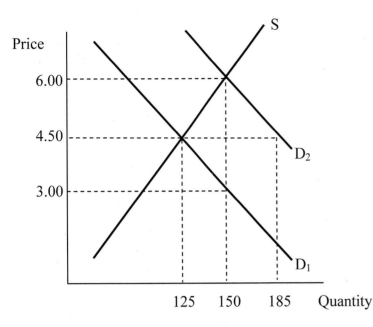

1.   An increase in demand from D₁ to D₂ would cause the equilibrium price in this market to:
       a. rise from $4.50 to $6.00, while the equilibrium quantity would rise from 125 to 150.
       b. rise from $4.50 to $6.00, while the equilibrium quantity would rise from 150 to 185.
       c. fall from $6.00 to $4.50, while the equilibrium quantity would fall from 150 to 125.
       d. fall from $6.00 to $4.50, while the equilibrium quantity would fall from 185 to 150.

2.   If the current demand curve is shown by D₂ and the current price is $4.50, then:
       a. there is excess supply equal to 60 units.
       b. there is excess demand equal to 60 units.
       c. there is excess supply equal to 30 units.
       d. there is excess demand equal to 30 units.

3.   The shift from D₁ to D₂ was most likely caused by:
       a. an increase in the price of this product from $4.50 to $6.00.
       b. a decrease in the price of this product from $6.00 to $4.50.
       c. an increase in consumer income or in the number of consumers in this market.
       d. a decrease in the cost of producing this product.

4.   If the current price in the market for applesauce is above the equilibrium price, then:
       a. there is excess supply of applesauce, so the price is likely to rise.
       b. there is excess supply of applesauce, so the price is likely to fall.
       c. there is excess demand for applesauce, so the price is likely to rise.
       d. there is excess demand for applesauce, so the price is likely to fall.

5.   If the current price in the market for applesauce is below the equilibrium price, then:
      a. there is excess supply of applesauce, so the price is likely to rise.
      b. there is excess supply of applesauce, so the price is likely to fall.
      c. there is excess demand for applesauce, so the price is likely to rise.
      d. there is excess demand for applesauce, so the price is likely to fall.

6.   When storeowners are left with unsold goods, they usually:
      a. raise the price of their goods to eliminate the excess supply.
      b. raise the price of their goods to eliminate the excess demand.
      c. lower the price of their goods to eliminate the excess supply.
      d. lower the price of their goods to eliminate the excess demand.

7.   When storeowners realize their goods are selling faster than their ability to stock them, they usually:
      a. raise the price of their goods to eliminate the excess supply.
      b. raise the price of their goods to eliminate the excess demand.
      c. lower the price of their goods to eliminate the excess supply.
      d. lower the price of their goods to eliminate the excess demand.

8.   If supply and demand intersect at a price of $3.50, then at a price of $5.25 there will be:
      a. a balance between supply and demand because demand will increase.
      b. a balance between supply and demand because supply will decrease.
      c. an excess supply.
      d. an excess demand.

9.   If supply and demand intersect at a price of $3.50, then at a price of $2.25 there will be:
      a. a balance between supply and demand because demand will decrease.
      b. a balance between supply and demand because supply will increase.
      c. an excess supply.
      d. an excess demand.

10.   When the market is in equilibrium:
      a. sellers are dissatisfied with the price being charged because there is neither excess demand nor excess supply.
      b. sellers want to raise the price being charged to eliminate the excess demand.
      c. sellers want to lower the price being charged to eliminate the excess supply.
      d. it is not possible for sellers to change the price being charged.

4.4   Graphing Problems

1.   Use the data below to answer the questions.

Price	Quantity Demanded	Quantity Supplied
$1.00	500	200
$1.25	450	250
$1.50	400	300
$1.75	350	350
$2.00	300	400

a)   Plot the points of the Demand curve and the points of the Supply curve in the space below. Connect the points of each curve and label them as D (for demand) and S (for supply).

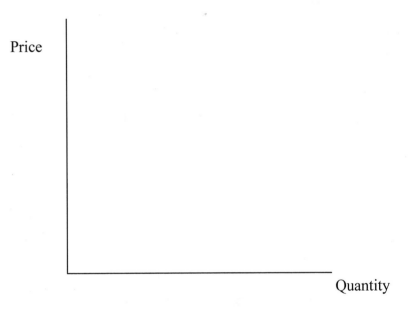

b)   Suppose the current price charged for this product is $1.25. How many units will consumers be willing and able to purchase at that price? How many units will firms be willing and able to sell at that price? Is there excess supply or excess demand? If so, how much?

c)   Suppose the current price charged for this product is $2.00. How many units will consumers be willing and able to purchase at that price? How many units will firms be willing and able to sell at that price? Is there excess supply or excess demand? If so, how much?

d)   What will be the equilibrium price and quantity in this market? Explain how you know.

2.   Sketch supply and demand graphs to illustrate the effects of each of the following events on equilibrium price and quantity:

a) The market for watermelons is in equilibrium initially. Then, consumer income increases and consumers decide that they like watermelon more than before.

b) The market for cell phone service is in equilibrium initially. Then, technology improves, causing the cost of providing service to cell phone customers to drop.

c) The market for overnight deliveries is in equilibrium initially. Then, the wages paid to delivery drivers increases, causing the costs of making deliveries to rise.

The Answer Key

4.1   True/False: 1. T 2. F 3. T 4. T 5. F 6. T 7. T 8. F 9. F 10. T

4.2   Multiple Choice: 1. A 2. A 3. C 4. B 5. D 6. C 7. A 8. C 9. D 10. D

4.3   Find your answers

4.4   Graphing Problems:
1. a) The graph should show a linear, downward-sloping demand curve and a linear, upward-sloping supply curve. b) The quantity demanded = 450 and the quantity supplied = 250, so there is excess demand = 200. c) The quantity demanded = 300 and the quantity supplied = 400, so there is excess supply = 100. d) Equilibrium occurs where Demand and Supply intersect, price = $1.75 and quantity = 350.
2. a) The demand curve is shifting to the right, causing equilibrium price and quantity to rise. b) The supply curve is shifting to the right, causing equilibrium price to fall and equilibrium quantity to rise. c) The supply curve is shifting to the left, causing equilibrium price to rise and equilibrium quantity to fall.

CHAPTER 5: THE CLASSICAL MACRO MODEL

Key Concepts

Aggregate Demand (AD) equals the sum of expenditures undertaken by consumers (C), investors (I), and the government (G) on domestically produced goods and services. In symbols

$$AD = C + I + G + X - M$$

where X stands for exports and M for imports, and all values are expressed in real terms.

Aggregate Supply (AS) is the real value of the revenue earned by all firms producing final goods and services.

The **Price Level** (P) is GDP deflator divided by 100.

Planned investment mainly equals real spending by businesses on capital goods and household spending on new residences. It also includes spending on the desired level of inventories but excludes any spending on unwanted inventories.

The **real rate** of interest equals the nominal or actual rate of interest minus the rate of inflation.

Say's Law argues that supply creates its own demand, so that no overproduction is ever possible.

Labor force includes anyone 16 and over and actively seeking a job. It excludes **discouraged workers**, i.e., those jobseekers who are so tired of looking for a job that they stop their job-search.

Seasonal unemployment occurs when the productive season expires for workers. Farm labor is a prime example here.

Frictional unemployment occurs when people move from one job to another and become temporarily jobless.

Voluntary unemployment occurs when people quit work because of the falling salary.

Structural unemployment occurs when someone's skills become outdated.

Natural unemployment includes seasonal, frictional, voluntary and structural unemployment.

Cyclical unemployment occurs when workers are laid off because of falling demand in some or all industries.

Full employment occurs when the official rate of unemployment is lower than or equal to the natural rate of unemployment, and the cyclical unemployment is absent.

The **rate of unemployment** is the percentage of those unemployed, i.e., it equals

$$\frac{(\text{ The number of the unemployed })}{\text{Labor Force}} \times 100$$

The **real wage** is money wage divided by the price level.

The **velocity of money (V)** is the number of times a dollar bill changes hands from buyers to various sellers.

Chapter Overview

Macro equilibrium occurs when

$$AD = AS,$$

or,

$$Y = AS = AD = C + I + G + X - M$$

With GDP equaling national income, all output ends up as someone's income, so that Y also equals real income. People use their incomes for consumption, paying net taxes (T) or saving (S), i.e.,

$$Y = C + S + T,$$

which in view of the above implies that

$$C + S + T = C + I + G + X - M$$

Or

$$S + T + M = I + G + X$$

Here T includes taxes net of government's transfer payments. Assuming that the government budget and foreign trade are balanced, so that $T = G$, and $X = M$,

$$S = I.$$

Thus in simplified macro equilibrium with balanced budget and trade, three conditions are satisfied.

- i. AD = AS
- *ii.* *I = S*
- iii. Unwanted inventory investments or unsold goods are zero

Say's law and the classical theory of the rate of interest ensure that in the long run there is no overproduction or unwanted inventory investment. According to classical economists, savings are positively linked to the real rate of interest, and investment is negatively linked to this rate. The real rate of interest moves up or down to bring about the equality of savings and investment.

According to the classical theory of employment, there is an automatic mechanism in a free market-economy that ensures full employment, as defined above, so that labor demand equals labor supply at the prevailing wage rate. This mechanism has two prongs: First, the real wage flexibility brings about an equality between labor demand and labor supply. Second, the interest-rate flexibility ensures that all output produced by the fully-employed labor force is sold, so that AD =AS, and there are no unwanted inventories.

The price level (P) establishes the link between real and nominal variables. In the classical model, the **quantity theory of money** determines P. because

$$MV = PY$$

where P is the price level, Y the aggregate supply or real GDP, M the supply of money, and V, the income velocity of money. Here

$$Y = AL$$

and $A = Y/L$ is the average product of employed labor (L).

According to classical economists, all unemployment is voluntary. The classical model offers the following prescriptions:

- (1) No minimum wage
- (2) No monetary policy
- (3) No government budget deficit
- (4) Low taxation and hence low government spending

The classical model is illogical, because, contrary to its argument, there are no unused funds with banks even in a recession, so that the real rate of interest rate need not fall quickly. Secondly, the model requires investment to rise in recession, and that has never happened.

Keynes criticizes the classical theory of interest by arguing that firstly under some circumstances even a zero rate of interest may not eliminate overproduction, and secondly, the real wage may not fall sufficiently to eliminate unemployment.

The classical model has many logical flaws, and not surprisingly it is not a realistic model.

True-False Questions

5.1   Indicate whether the following statements are (T)rue or (F)alse:

_____ 1.   National demand is the purchasing power of total nominal spending in a nation.

_____ 2.   When an economy is in equilibrium, injections resulting from investment spending, government spending, and exports are equal to leakages.

_____ 3.   The main implication of Say's Law is that business firms react to overproduction by reducing output and laying off workers.

_____ 4.   If a lender charges a nominal interest rate of 10 percent and inflation turns out to be 4 percent, then the lender will earn 14 percent in real terms.

_____ 5.   There are only two reasons for unemployment according to the Classical model: unions and minimum wages.

_____ 6.   According to the Quantity Theory of Money, changes in the price level are the result of excessive money growth.

_____ 7.   According to the Quantity Theory of Money, real GDP and employment will both increase when the economy's supply of money is allowed to grow.

_____ 8.   The economy is at full employment if the officially estimated rate of unemployment is no larger than the natural rate, and there is no cyclical unemployment.

_____ 9.   Since business investment is most likely to expand during an economic downturn, a flexible real rate of interest guarantees that there will never be cyclical unemployment.

_____ 10.   A fall in nominal wages causes real wages to fall, regardless of what is happening to the price level.

5.2   **Multiple Choice** – circle the best response:

1.   Leakages of spending from the economy include:
      a. saving, investment, and exports.
      b. saving, taxes, and imports.
      c. investment, government spending, and imports.
      d. investment, government spending, and taxes.

2.   Injections of spending into the economy include:
     a. investment, taxes, and imports.
     b. investment, government spending, and exports.
     c. saving, taxes, and exports.
     d. saving, government spending, and imports.

3.   When leakages of spending from the economy are equal to injections of spending:
     a. aggregate spending exceeds aggregate production, so the price level rises.
     b. aggregate production exceeds aggregate spending, so the price level falls.
     c. aggregate demand and aggregate supply intersect, but the economy is not in equilibrium.
     d. aggregate demand and aggregate supply are equal and the economy is in equilibrium.

4.   When the economy is in equilibrium:
     a. there are no unintended inventories, so unsold goods do not pile up on store shelves.
     b. unintended inventory investment is equal to planned investment spending.
     c. unintended inventory investment is equal to saving.
     d. there are no leakages of spending from the economy.

5.   According to Say's Law:
     a. suppliers must believe that there is sufficient demand for their products before they will engage in the act of production.
     b. overproduction occurs when demand is weak and results in cyclical unemployment.
     c. the very act of production creates demand for goods made by others, so there can be no overproduction.
     d. individuals always consume the goods and services that they themselves produced.

6.   Suppose an economy with no foreign trade or government produces $500 worth of output and $500 worth of income for households. If households choose to spend $450 on goods for consumption, then:
     a. they will save $50, but there is no guarantee that businesses will borrow this entire amount to finance planned investments.
     b. they will save $50 and businesses will borrow $50 to finance planned investments.
     c. we cannot predict how much households will save based on the information provided.
     d. if households do not spend all of their income, then the economy will contract.

7.   Suppose an economy with no foreign trade or government produces $500 worth of output and $500 worth of income for households. If households choose to spend $450 on goods for consumption and businesses choose to borrow $42 to finance planned investments, then:
a. all of the goods produced will be purchased by consumers.
b. saving will equal planned investment.
c. there will be underproduction and depletion of inventories worth $8.
d. there will be overproduction and accumulation of unwanted inventories worth $8.

8.   You have agreed to give your brother a $1000 loan for one year. After one year, your brother will repay you $1080. If the price level has risen 3 percent between the time you made the loan and the time the loan was repaid, then you have earned:
a. an 8 percent nominal interest rate, but only a 5 percent real interest rate.
b. an 8 percent nominal interest rate, but only a 3 percent real interest rate.
c. a 5 percent nominal interest rate and an 8 percent real interest rate.
d. an 11 percent nominal interest rate, but only an 8 percent real interest rate.

9.   In an economy with inflation:
a. the real rate of interest is always less than the nominal rate of interest.
b. the real rate of interest is always greater than the nominal rate of interest.
c. the relationship between the real rate of interest and the nominal rate of interest cannot be predicted.
d. the real rate of interest will equal the nominal rate of interest as long as inflation was correctly predicted by lenders.

10.   According to the classical model, the interaction of supply and demand decisions in the loanable funds market determines the:
a. equilibrium rate of inflation.
b. equilibrium nominal rate of interest.
c. equilibrium real rate of interest.
d. amount of money that households will save independent of the rate of interest.

5.3   **Multiple Choice** – circle the best response:

1.   The investment demand curve is assumed to be:
a. upward-sloping because consumers save more when they earn a higher interest rate.
b. upward-sloping because consumers save less when they earn a higher interest rate.
c. downward-sloping because firms invest less at a lower interest fee.
d. downward-sloping because firms invest more at a lower interest fee.

2. The savings supply curve is assumed to be:
    a. upward-sloping because consumers save more when they earn a higher interest rate.
    b. upward-sloping because consumers save less when they earn a higher interest rate.
    c. downward-sloping because firms invest less at a lower interest fee.
    d. downward-sloping because firms invest more at a lower interest fee.

3. According to the classical model, if the current real interest rate is above the equilibrium rate, then:
    a. there will be excess demand in the loanable funds market and the rate will fall.
    b. there will be excess demand in the loanable funds market and the rate will rise.
    c. there will be excess supply in the loanable funds market and the rate will rise.
    d. there will be excess supply in the loanable funds market and the rate will fall.

4. According to the classical model, if the current real interest rate is below the equilibrium rate, then:
    a. there will be excess demand in the loanable funds market and the rate will fall.
    b. there will be excess demand in the loanable funds market and the rate will rise.
    c. there will be excess supply in the loanable funds market and the rate will rise.
    d. there will be excess supply in the loanable funds market and the rate will fall.

5. According to the classical model, if the current real wage rate is above the equilibrium rate, then:
    a. there will be excess demand in the labor market and the real wage will fall.
    b. there will be excess demand in the labor market and the real wage will rise.
    c. there will be excess supply in the labor market and the real wage will fall.
    d. there will be excess supply in the labor market and the real wage will rise.

6. The two pillars in the classical framework are:
    a. unions and minimum wage legislation.
    b. real wage flexibility and real interest rate flexibility.
    c. leakages and injections.
    d. cyclical unemployment and recessions.

7. According to the quantity theory of money, if the economy is at full employment and monetary authorities increase the economy's supply of money, then:
    a. the price level will increase with no change in output or employment.
    b. velocity will fall and nominal GDP will be unaffected.
    c. the price level will increase, output will increase, and employment will increase.
    d. real GDP will increase and the price level will fall.

8.   When workers lose their jobs because technological change has made their skills obsolete, their unemployment is termed:
      a. structural, and is eliminated as soon as they acquire new skills.
      b. frictional, and is eliminated as soon as they complete their job search.
      c. seasonal, and the unemployment episode will end when the season changes.
      d. cyclical, and can never be eliminated.

9.   The most important difference between cyclical unemployment and the other types of unemployment is that:
      a. there is not type of government policy that can eliminate cyclical unemployment.
      b. when there is cyclical unemployment, there are not enough job vacancies to accommodate all of the unemployment workers.
      c. when there is cyclical unemployment, there are plenty of job vacancies but workers will have to retrain or relocate to find jobs.
      d. structural and frictional unemployment are very rare, while cyclical unemployment is commonplace.

10.   The economy is considered to be at full employment when:
      a. the natural rate of unemployment is below 3 percent.
      b. the actual unemployment rate is equal to the natural rate, about 5 percent.
      c. the actual unemployment rate is below the natural rate.
      d. there are no officially unemployed workers.

5.4   Graphing Questions

1.   Use the graph to answer the questions below.

Real Interest Rate

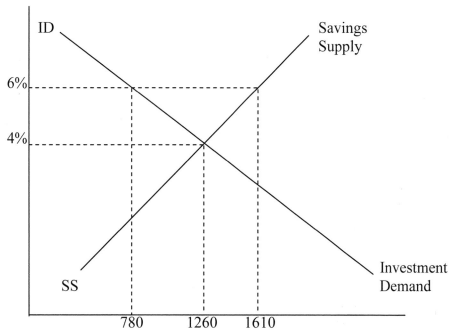

a)   If the real interest rate is currently 6%, how much are households saving? How much are businesses borrowing to finance planned investments? What is the value of unintended inventory investment in this case?

b)   According to the classical model, what would motivate lenders to lower the real interest rate from 6% to 4%?

c) Suppose businesses are borrowing $830 billion to finance unintended inventories at a real interest rate of 6%. In this case, do you think it likely that lenders will find it necessary to immediately lower rates from 6% to 4%? Explain.

2. Use the graph to answer the questions below.

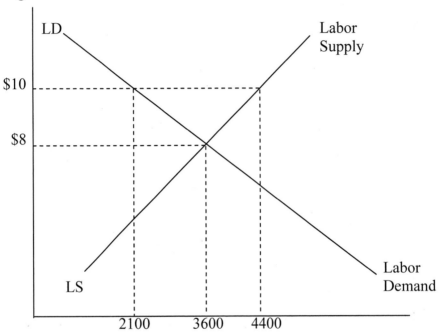

a) According to the classical model, what are the only possible explanations for the real wage being "stuck" at $10?

b) If the real wage rate is $10, how many labor hours will employers demand? How many labor hours will be supplied by workers?

c)   Explain how this market would achieve equilibrium assuming the real wage is perfectly flexible. What does this imply about the existence of long-term unemployment?

5.5   **Discussion Questions**

1.   Explain why Say's Law implies that the economy will always be in equilibrium at full employment.

2.   What are the two pillars of the classical framework?

3.   Define and give examples of seasonal unemployment, frictional unemployment, and structural unemployment.

4.   Explain why the economy is said to be operating at full employment even when the rate of unemployment is in the 4 to 6 percent range.

5.   What are some of the specific policy prescriptions offered by the classical model?

6.   What were the assumptions underlying classical theory that were criticized by John Maynard Keynes?

The Answer Key

5.1   True/False: 1. T 2. T 3. F 4. F 5. T 6. T 7. F 8. T 9. F 10. F

5.2   Multiple Choice: 1. B 2. B 3. D 4. A 5. C 6. A 7. D 8. A 9. A 10.C

5.3   Find your answers

5.4   Graphing Questions:
   1. a) Households save $1,610 billion and businesses borrow $780 billion to finance planned investments; unintended inventory investment is $830 billion. b) At a real interest rate of 6%, there is an excess supply of loanable funds. If lenders can't find anyone to borrow these funds at 6%, they will lower the rate until they can find willing and qualified borrowers. c) As long as total borrowing is $1,610 billion ($780 billion for planned investments and $830 billion to pay for unplanned inventories), there is no excess supply and no motivation for lenders to lower rates.
   2. a) Union contracts and minimum wage legislation can keep the wage "stuck" above equilibrium. b) Employers demand 2,100 million labor hours and workers supply 4,400 million labor hours at a real wage of $10. c) There is a large amount of excess supply (unemployed workers) at the real wage of $10; unemployed workers will accept pay cuts, causing the market to move toward equilibrium. This model implies that unemployment can never by a long-term problem in an economy with perfectly flexible (real) wages.

5.5   Discussion Questions: 1. See page 81 of text. 2. See page 86 of text. 3. See pages 89-90 of text. 4. See page 91 of text. 5. See page 92 of text. 6. See page 101 of text.

CHAPTER 6: THE NEOCLASSICAL MODEL

Key Concepts

Marginal Product of Labor (MPL) is the increase in output that occurs when a firm hires another worker, while keeping other factors of production, mainly capital, constant. The MPL eventually declines as more labor is hired. This is known as the **law of diminishing MPL**.

Average product of labor (APL) is the average output of all workers. In the economy as a whole, the MPL is less than the APL, and the difference is the marginal product of capital.

Supply Shocks are the disturbances that hit the supply side of an economy. They include climatic changes, oil price increases, technological developments, marginal income tax rates, raw material prices, among others.

Intertemporal Substitution occurs when a worker decides to postpone working in anticipation of higher income in the future.

Chapter Overview

The neoclassical model improves upon the classical inability to explain the recessionary part of the business cycle, and generally opposes government activism to eradicate joblessness. The labor market in this view always remains at full employment, while the minimum-wage law hurts the workers by increasing unemployment.

Variations in real GDP and employment reflect the free choices of workers. Employment and output decrease whenever people choose to withhold their labor from employers, and soar whenever households rush into the labor force because of higher wages and interest rates or lower income taxes. The neoclassical model insists that this is primarily the way in which the business cycle has operated in U.S. history.

There was a time when neoclassical economists vehemently opposed the government budget deficit, but in support of President George W. Bush and his multitude of tax-cut plans, they have recently mellowed and abandoned their passion. They now favor an income tax reduction regardless of the cost to future generations, who will have to pay off the government debt.

True-False Questions

6.1   Indicate whether the following statements are (T)rue or (F)alse:

_____ 1.   If the marginal product of the sixth worker is 10 units of output and each of those units can be sold for $1.50, then a firm would definitely hire the sixth worker.

_____ 2.   A profit-maximizing employer, facing perfect competition, will continue to hire workers up to the point where the wage is equal to the product price multiplied by the marginal product of labor.

_____ 3.   The law of diminishing marginal product means that if a firm were to double all of its inputs, total output would less than double.

_____ 4.   If capital stock is held constant, the marginal product of labor will eventually decline as more workers are hired.

_____ 5.   If the marginal product of labor is less than the average product of labor, then the average product of labor is necessarily falling.

_____ 6.   The marginal product of labor curve is the neoclassical labor demand curve, because at each equilibrium point MPL equals the real wage.

_____ 7.   The neoclassical labor supply curve is positively sloped, indicating that a higher real wage attracts more people in the job market or induces some to work more hours.

_____ 8.   In the neoclassical framework, labor supply is assumed to be independent of tax rates and the real interest rate.

_____ 9.   The neoclassical aggregate supply curve is vertical because the economy is assumed to always operate at the full employment level of real GDP.

_____ 10.   Neoclassical economists use the concept of intertemporal substitution to explain why workers sometimes choose to be unemployed.

True-False Questions

6.2   Indicate whether the following statements are (T)rue or (F)alse:

_____   1.   According to real business cycle theorists, most economic downturns can be explained by negative aggregate supply shifts.

_____   2.   The most important criticism of the real business cycle model is that it does not permit fluctuations in output or employment.

_____   3.   Supply-side economists believe that any government policy designed to improve the economy's performance is doomed to failure.

_____   4.   Supply-side economists believe the cure for joblessness lies in reducing corporate and individual tax rates to improve incentives to work and invest.

_____   5.   The Laffer curve is based on the notion that lower tax rates will actually cause tax revenues to increase due to improved incentives on the supply side.

_____   6.   The most important criticism of the supply-side model is that it ignores the effect of tax cuts on the government's budget.

_____   7.   If the federal government simultaneously lowers taxes and borrows funds to cover its budget deficit, then the overall effect is to stimulate spending and employment.

_____   8.   In the neoclassical model, joblessness is the outcome of a worker's free choice to offer labor services only when the real wage rate is sufficiently high.

_____   9.   Robert Lucas, 1995 Nobel laureate, argues that workers would never leave their jobs voluntarily because this would threaten the workers' survival.

_____   10.   In a 1996 survey, a majority of workers reported that they would be willing to get more training, work longer hours, and even accept pay cuts in order to keep their jobs.

6.3   **Multiple Choice** – circle the best response:

1.   The neoclassical condition for labor market equilibrium is:
a. marginal product of labor (MPL) = zero.
b. marginal product of labor (MPL) = nominal wage (W).
c. marginal product of labor (MPL) = real wage (W/P).
d. real wage (W/P) = nominal wage (W).

2.   In the neoclassical model, an increase in the supply of labor causes:
a. both the nominal wage and the price level to fall by the same proportion.
b. both the nominal wage and the price level to rise by the same proportion.
c. the real wage to fall.
d. the real wage to rise.

3.   The neoclassical aggregate supply curve is:
a. upward-sloping because an increase in the real interest rate causes an increase in labor supply.
b. upward-sloping because the labor force is fixed and always fully employed.
c. vertical because an increase in the real interest rate causes an increase in labor supply.
d. vertical because the labor force is fixed and always fully employed.

4.   Real business cycle theorists believe that recessions are:
a. caused by a leftward shift of the aggregate supply curve.
b. caused by a rightward shift of the aggregate supply curve.
c. impossible because the economy always operates at full employment.
d. possible in the short run because real wages are not fully flexible.

5.   Supply-side economists believe that recessions:
a. can be cured by lowering income and corporate tax rates.
b. cannot be cured using any type of government policy.
c. never happen, so no policy cure is called for.
d. can be cured using policies that encourage people to spend more.

6.   The classical and neoclassical models:
a. do not share a common ideology.
b. are virtually identical in explaining macroeconomic phenomenon.
c. both advocate a laissez faire approach to economic policy.
d. both advocate government intervention designed to improve the economy's performance.

7. The oil price shocks of the 1970s:
    a. provide irrefutable proof that the real business cycle model is valid.
    b. were not a very good test of the real business cycle model because it does not attempt to explain supply shocks.
    c. supported the prediction made by the real business cycle model that negative supply shocks will lead to higher unemployment, but did not support the prediction that real GDP will decline.
    d. did not support the predictions of the real business cycle model very well.

8. The intertemporal substitution effect implies that when real wages fall:
    a. firms will choose to increase the quantity of labor demanded.
    b. firms will choose to reduce the quantity of labor demanded.
    c. workers will choose to increase the quantity of labor supplied.
    d. workers will choose to reduce the quantity of labor supplied.

9. "All joblessness is by choice" is consistent with all of the following models except:
    a. the Keynesian model.
    b. Supply-side economics.
    c. the neoclassical model.
    d. real business cycle theory.

10. According to a 1996 survey on workers' willingness to make concessions to their employers:
    a. workers who have been laid off report they would have made concessions to keep their jobs, but those who remain employed do not report any willingness to make concessions.
    b. the majority of workers are willing to make a number of concessions in order to keep their jobs.
    c. workers would clearly rather lose their jobs than accept pay cuts.
    d. there is strong evidence that all unemployment is voluntary.

6.4   Graphing Questions

1.   Use the graph to answer the questions below.

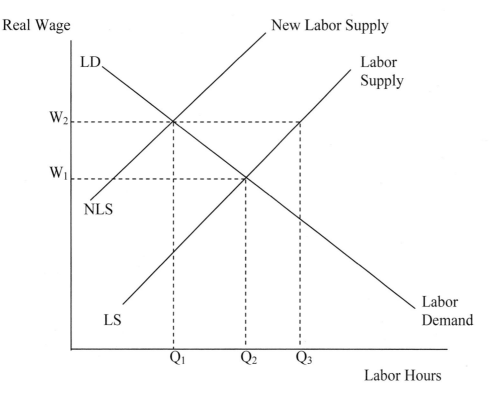

a)   List some events that might be responsible for the leftward shift of the labor supply curve shown above.

b)   Suppose the labor market is initially in equilibrium at a real wage of W_1 and quantity of labor hours Q_2. According to neoclassical economists, what will happen to the real wage and the quantity of labor hours if government imposes higher income tax rates? Will this lead to unemployment? Explain.

c)   Explain how this model can explain declining real GDP during a recession, but not increasing unemployment. Does historical evidence support the predictions of this model?

2. **Use the graph to answer the questions below.**

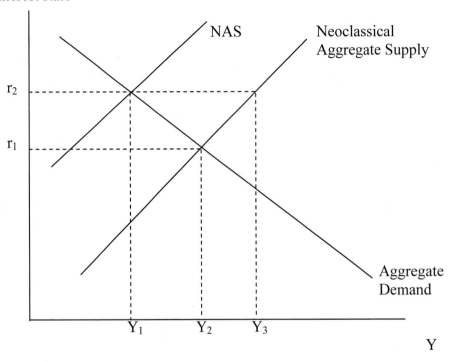

Real Interest Rate

NAS

Neoclassical
Aggregate Supply

r_2

r_1

Aggregate
Demand

Y_1 Y_2 Y_3

Y

a) List some events that might be responsible for the left ward shift of the aggregate supply curve shown above.

b) According to this graph, what will happen to output (Y) following a negative supply shift?

c) Does declining output necessarily mean rising unemployment? What must be assumed about joblessness to reconcile declining output with a constant rate of unemployment?

6.5   Problems/Discussion Questions

1.   What is the relationship between the marginal product of labor (MPL) and the demand for labor curve? If a firm must pay workers a wage of $10 per hour to produce goods that sell in the market for $2 each, will the firm hire a third worker if the marginal product of the third worker is 6 units of output? Explain how you know.

2.   In the Neoclassical model, what is the relationship between income tax rates and worker effort? What is the relationship between the real interest rate and worker effort? Explain what happens to labor supply as a result of an increase in income tax rates or a decrease in the real interest rate in this model.

3.   Summarize the explanation for changes in employment and real GDP offered by Real Business Cycle theorists.

4.   If government reduces income and corporate taxes, and then borrows money to cover the resulting budget deficit, what is this likely to do to saving, investment, and economic growth?

5.   Use examples to explain the difference between voluntary unemployment and involuntary unemployment. Which of these is the only kind assumed to occur in the Neoclassical model?

The Answer Key

6.1   True/False: 1. F 2. T 3. F 4. T 5. T 6. T 7. T 8. F 9. F 10. T

6.2   Find your answers

6.3   Multiple Choice: 1. C 2. C 3. A 4. A 5. A 6. C 7. D 8. D 9. A 10. B

6.4   Graphing Questions:
   1. a) In the neoclassical framework, higher income taxes and lower real interest rates reduce work incentives and cause the labor supply to shift leftward. b) The equilibrium real wage rises and the equilibrium quantity of labor falls; this does not lead to unemployment because the leftward shift of the labor supply function corresponds to a choice by workers to reduce work effort. c) The fall in labor supply causes output to fall, but there is no unemployment because the decision not to work is voluntary; historically, recessions have been characterized by both falling real GDP and increasing unemployment, so this prediction is not realistic.
   2. a) In the neoclassical model, aggregate supply shifts to the left due to changes in preferences (regarding saving and work effort) and higher input prices, for example.
   b) Output falls as a result of this shift. c) The model predicts that output will fall and fewer people will have jobs, but that this joblessness is voluntary so there is no cyclical unemployment.

Problems/Discussion Questions:

1. They are the same. Yes, the cost of hiring the worker ($10) is less than the benefit ($2 x 6 = $12).
2. See pages 108-109 of text.
3. See pages 111-114 of text.
4. See page 116 of text.
5. See page 120 of text.

CHAPTER 7: THE KEYNESIAN MODEL

Key Concepts

The Consumption function describes a positive relationship between a nation's GDP or income and aggregate consumer spending.

The Saving function describes a positive relationship between a nation's GDP or income and aggregate savings.

The marginal propensity to consume is the fraction of new income consumed.

The marginal propensity to save is the fraction of new income saved.

Autonomous consumption is consumer spending not linked to national income or GDP.

Autonomous investment is investment not linked to GDP or national income.

GDP Multiplier is the effect of any change in autonomous spending on real GDP.

The autonomous budget deficit is the government's excess of its spending over tax revenue unrelated to GDP.

Production Function describes the state of technology that links factors of production to output.

Fiscal policy is the government's setting of its tax rates and levels of spending to achieve full employment and price stability.

Monetary policy is the regulation of the nation's money supply by the central bank to achieve full employment and price stability.

True inflation is the jump in prices that may occur after the country attains full employment.

Transactions demand for money is the quantity of money people keep as cash or in checking accounts to carry out day-to-day transactions.

Precautionary demand for money is the quantity of money people keep as cash or in checking accounts to meet financial emergencies.

Speculative demand for money is the quantity of money people keep in savings accounts to buy income earning assets, such as stocks and bonds, in the future.

Liquidity trap is the state of an economy where the rate of interest has fallen to its minimum, close to zero, so that no amount of monetary stimulus can lower it significantly.

Chapter Overview

Keynesian economics is the anti-thesis of classical economics. Deficiency of aggregate demand results in involuntary or cyclical unemployment, which occurs when job seekers exceed vacancies prevailing at the market real and money wage.

The Great Depression occurred in the United States, because the fall in investment following the stock market crash led to a sharp decrease in aggregate demand. It was made worse by a falling money wage and a perverse fiscal policy that sharply raised the income tax on all sections of society. In macro equilibrium, real GDP equals autonomous spending times the multiplier. The multiplier is the inverse of the marginal propensity to save.

The marginal propensity to consume (mpc) establishes a link between national income and consumer spending. An initial fall in spending produces a greater fall in aggregate demand because of the multiplier, so that even a small investment decline may cause a large decline in output and employment.

The rate of interest is determined in the money market by the twin forces of money demand and money supply. Money demand falls with a rise in the interest rate but rises with a rise in nominal GDP. A rise in money supply generates a fall in the interest rate, except when the economy is in the **liquidity trap**, where the interest rate has already reached its minimum.

Expansionary fiscal policy that calls for a large government budget deficit is the best cure for a depression. Both types of expansionary policies— monetary as well as fiscal—can be effective in a recession.

A **progressive tax system** raises the marginal propensity to consume, and may produce a moderate increase in employment without a budget deficit. Fiscal and monetary policies should be contractionary in the case of inflation.

Important Formulas

Consumption Function: $\qquad C = C^* + mpc \cdot Y$

$$mpc = \frac{\Delta C}{\Delta Y} \leq 1$$

$$mps = \frac{\Delta S}{\Delta Y} = 1 - mpc,$$

Aggregate Demand: $\quad\quad AD = C + I = C* + \text{mpc} \cdot Y + I*$

Equilibrium GDP: $\quad\quad\quad Y = \dfrac{C*+I*}{1- mpc}$

$$= \dfrac{A*}{mps}$$

where $A* = C* + I*$ is total autonomous spending. Thus, *in equilibrium GDP equals total autonomous spending divided by the marginal propensity to save.*

$$\textbf{GDP multiplier} = \dfrac{1}{mps}$$

$$GDP = A* \cdot \text{multiplier}$$

In the presence of the government's budget deficit, $A* = C* + I* + B*$, where B* is the government's budget deficit.

Change in GDP: $\quad\quad\quad \Delta GDP = \Delta A* \cdot \text{multiplier}$

Desired Change in Budget Deficit: $\quad \Delta B* = \dfrac{\Delta GDP}{multiplier}$

Production Function: $\quad\quad\quad Y = F(Ko, L)$

where *Ko* is the fixed stock of capital and *L* is employment.

Labor-Market Equilibrium: $\quad\quad$ money wage $=$ price level $\times$ MPL
$$= P \cdot \text{MPL}$$

Money Demand Function: $\quad\quad MD = kPY - qi$

Investment Function: $\quad\quad\quad I = I* - hi,$

The last expression is known as the investment function. Investment now has two components, one autonomous ($I*$), and the other linked negatively to the rate of interest (i). Here h is a known number that links the rate of interest to the level of investment spending, and the minus sign indicates that the relationship is negative; k and q are known numbers that respectively link money demand (MD) to nominal GDP, equaling PY, and the rate of interest (i). The equation shows that the rate of interest has a negative influence on MD, whereas nominal GDP has a positive influence.

True-False Questions

<u>7.1</u>   Indicate whether the following statements are (T)rue or (F)alse:

_____ 1.   In the Keynesian consumption equation, the marginal propensity to consume (mpc) is constant and less than one.

_____ 2.   If the marginal propensity to consume (mpc) is equal to 0.95, then the marginal propensity to save (mps) is equal to 0.05.

_____ 3.   If a component of spending is "autonomous", then its value is determined by solving the model.

_____ 4.   Given a simplified model with no government, no foreign spending, fixed prices, and assuming that national income and GDP are equal, equilibrium GDP equals total autonomous spending divided by the marginal propensity to save (mps).

_____ 5.   In the Classical framework, there is no direct role for the labor market in generating equilibrium GDP.

_____ 6.   In the Keynesian framework, supply plays a passive role with output determined by aggregate demand.

_____ 7.   In the Classical model, equilibrium GDP is unique because the supply of labor is invariant to the interest rate.

_____ 8.   In the Keynesian model, equilibrium GDP is unique because aggregate demand always intersects the 45 degree line at a fixed level of output.

_____ 9.   In the Keynesian model with no government or foreign sector, income changes until savings is equal to investment.

_____ 10.   The paradox of thrift refers to the fact that a higher level of savings is the only way to cause GDP to increase, yet consumers refuse to save enough to guarantee economic prosperity.

True-False Questions

7.2   Indicate whether the following statements are (T)rue or (F)alse:

_____ 1.   The smaller the marginal propensity to save (mps), the larger the size of the GDP multiplier.

_____ 2.   If the marginal propensity to save (mps) is 0.05, then the multiplier is equal to 20 even if taxes and imports cause leakages from the spending stream.

_____ 3.   Because of the multiplier effect, a change in autonomous spending generates a larger change in equilibrium output.

_____ 4.   Keynes argued that the recession of 1929 began with a fall in investment spending resulting from the uncertainty created by the stock market crash.

_____ 5.   The GDP multiplier does not play a significant role in Keynesian economics.

_____ 6.   The balanced budget multiplier is equal to one, regardless of the size of the marginal propensity to save (mps).

_____ 7.   The law of diminishing marginal product implies that the production function for a typical economy is linear with respect to labor employment.

_____ 8.   In the Keynesian model, full employment occurs only if the demand determined output is large enough to absorb all the job seekers ready to accept the prevailing wage.

_____ 9.   Since money earns little or no interest, rational people will never choose to hold any of their assets in the form of money.

_____ 10.   Keynes advocated the use of expansionary fiscal policy to cure a depression, with the resulting budget deficits balanced against budgetary surpluses accumulated during years of economic prosperity.

7.3   **Multiple Choice** – circle the best response:

1.   Keynes did not agree with the Classical view that:
      a. the interest rate is the chief determinant of consumption and savings.
      b. income is the chief determinant of consumption and savings.
      c. the economy will break down if firms are unable to sell all of the output produced.
      d. consumption and saving decisions are independent of one another.

2.   If $C = 400 + 0.8(Y)$, where C = consumption spending and Y = income, then autonomous consumption is equal to:
      a. 0.8.
      b. 0.2.
      c. 400.
      d. 2,000.

3.   If $C = 400 + 0.8(Y)$, where C = consumption spending and Y = income, then the marginal propensity to consume (mpc) is equal to:
      a. 0.8.
      b. 0.2.
      c. 400.
      d. 2,000.

4.   If $C = 400 + 0.8(Y)$, where C = consumption spending and Y = income, then the marginal propensity to save (mps) is equal to:
      a. 0.8.
      b. 0.2.
      c. 400.
      d. 2,000.

5.   If $C = 400 + 0.8(Y)$, where C = consumption spending and Y = income, then the breakeven level of income is equal to:
      a. 0.8.
      b. 0.2.
      c. 400.
      d. 2,000.

6.   If C = 400 + 0.8(Y), where C = consumption spending and Y = income, and
      autonomous investment spending (I*) is equal to 600, then equilibrium income in
      an economy with no government, no foreign spending, and fixed prices is:
      a. $2,000.
      b. $3,000.
      c. $4,000.
      d. $5,000.

7.   In the Classical framework:
      a. there is no direct role for the labor market in generating equilibrium GDP.
      b. the labor market plays a direct role in generating equilibrium GDP.
      c. equilibrium GDP is determined by the strength of aggregate demand (AD).
      d. spending and saving decisions affect the level of production and employment,
         but not the price level.

8.   In the Keynesian Cross diagram:
      a. there can only be one equilibrium value for GDP and it is determined by
         aggregate supply (AS).
      b. any equilibrium point must lie on the 45 degree line.
      c. a change in autonomous spending will change the economy's equilibrium GDP.
      d. (b) and (c) are both true.

9.   The economy's equilibrium level of output:
      a. will fluctuate in the Classical model due to changes in labor supply.
      b. does not fluctuate in the Neoclassical model.
      c. will fluctuate in the Keynesian model due to changes in aggregate demand.
      d. all of the above are true.

10.   In the Keynesian model with no government or foreign sector, if households choose to
      save $800 at the current level of income and autonomous investment spending is equal to
      $600, then:
      a. the interest rate will fall, causing saving to fall until it is equal to investment.
      b. the interest rate will fall, causing investment to rise until it is equal to savings.
      c. income will fall, causing savings to fall until it is equal to investment.
      d. income will rise, causing investment to rise until it is equal to savings.

7.4   **Multiple Choice** – circle the best response:

1.   If total government spending exceeds total government income, then:
a. the government has a balanced budget.
b. the government has a budget deficit.
c. the government has a budget surplus.
d. there is not enough information to determine the state of the government's
    budget.

2.   Suppose autonomous consumption (C*) = 250, autonomous investment spending (I*) = 590, and the government has a budget deficit (B*) = 160.   Then, total autonomous spending is equal to:
a. $840.
b. $1,000.
c. $1,250.
d. $1,590.

3.   Suppose autonomous consumption (C*) = 250, autonomous investment spending (I*) = 590, and the government has a budget deficit (B*) = 160. If the GDP multiplier is 3, then equilibrium income and output in this economy will be:
a. $2,520.
b. $3,000.
c. $3,750.
d. $4,770.

4.   Keynes argued that the money wage is:
a. less stable than the real wage because the price level is fixed.
b. more stable than the real wage because the price level is fixed.
c. less stable than the real wage because workers resist pay cuts.
d. more stable than the real wage because workers resist pay cuts.

5.   In the Keynesian framework, joblessness:
a. can be either voluntary or involuntary, though the voluntary portion is relatively
    small.
b. can be either voluntary or involuntary, though the voluntary portion is always
    larger than the involuntary portion.
c. is always voluntary.
d. is always involuntary.

6.   The Keynesian model assumes that:
      a. the price level never changes.
      b. money wages never change.
      c. neither the price level nor money wages ever change.
      d. increases in spending can cause both the price level and the money wage to
         rise.

7.   Fiscal policy involves:
      a. adjustment of government spending and/or taxes.
      b. regulations that limit the profitability of corporations.
      c. changes in the money supply and interest rates.
      d. adjustment of the tax code to ensure fairness.

8.   Keynesian economics recommends:
      a. allowing the government to incur budget deficits year after year.
      b. requiring that the government maintain a balanced budget each year.
      c. permitting budget deficits during recessionary periods, but balancing these
         against budget surpluses during inflationary periods.
      d. permitting budget surpluses during recessionary periods, but balancing these
         against budget deficits during inflationary periods.

9.   If the government raises taxes on the rich by $100 and lowers taxes on the poor
      by $100, then:
      a. there can be no change in total spending nor any effect on income distribution.
      b. there can be no change in total spending, but the distribution of income will be
         changed.
      c. there will likely be an increase in spending because the poor will spend the
         entire tax cut, whereas the extra taxes paid by the rich have little effect on their
         spending.
      d. there will likely be a decrease in spending because the rich would have spent
         the money paid in taxes, whereas the poor will not spend the tax cut.

10.   If there is a liquidity trap, then:
      a. expansionary monetary policy is useless because no amount of monetary
         expansion will reduce the interest rate.
      b. contractionary monetary policy is useless because no amount of monetary
         contraction will raise the interest rate.
      c. expansionary fiscal policy is useless because no amount of government
         spending will increase aggregate demand.
      d. contractionary fiscal policy is useless because no amount of tax increases
         will reduce aggregate demand.

7.5   Problems

1.   Given the Consumption function   C = 225 + 0.75(Y_D), where C is consumption spending and Y_D is Disposable Income, sketch a graph of this function in the space below and fill in the missing values.

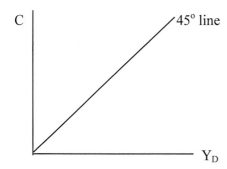

autonomous consumption = _____

marginal propensity to consume (mpc) = _____

marginal propensity to save (mps) = _____

Breakeven Disposable Income = _____

2.   Given: C = 400 + 0.75(Y) and I = 750, where C is consumption spending, Y is Income, and I is investment spending. Use this model of spending behavior to fill in the missing values.

Equilibrium income (Y) and output = _____. If full-employment real GDP is $5,000, then

this economy will be _____. Investment spending would have to increase by
                        in a recession/booming

_____ in order to have equilibrium output equal to full-employment output. The GDP

multiplier in this case is equal to _____.

7.6   **Graphing Questions** – use the graph below to fill in the blanks.

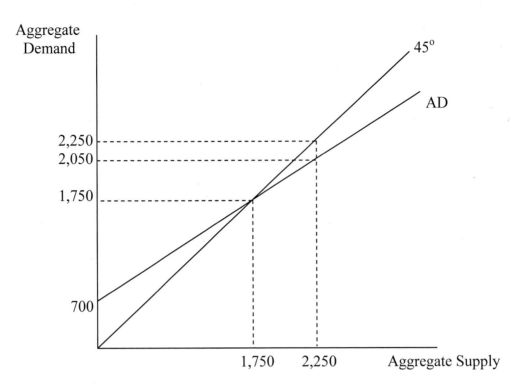

1.   Total autonomous spending is equal to _____.

2.   The marginal propensity to consume (mps) is equal to _____.

3.   The marginal propensity to save (mps) is equal to _____.

4.   Equilibrium income and output is equal to _____.

5.   If $2,250 worth of output is produced, spending will fall short of output by _____.

7.7   Discussion Questions

1.   Summarize the Classical response to the Great Depression.

2.   Explain why the Keynesian equilibrium is stable.

3.   What is the Paradox of Thrift? What is the significance of this paradox?

4.   If demand-determined output is large enough to absorb all of the job seekers ready to accept the prevailing wage, then the economy will operate at full employment. According to Keynes, why doesn't the prevailing wage simply adjust until firms are willing to hire all available workers?

5.   In the Keynesian framework, is joblessness always voluntary? Explain.

6.   Money earns little or no interest, yet people are willing to hold money even when they could choose income-yielding assets like stocks or bonds. According to Keynes, what are the three motives for money demand? Briefly describe each of these.

The Answer Key

7.1   True/False: 1. T 2. T 3. F 4. T 5. F 6. T 7. T 8. F 9. T 10. F

7.2   Find your answers

7.3   Multiple Choice: 1. A 2. C 3. A 4. B 5. D 6. D 7. B 8. D 9. C 10. C

7.4   Find your answers

7.5   Problems: 1. 225; 0.75; 0.25; 900. 2. 4600; in a recession; 100; 4.

7.6   Graphing Questions: 1. 700. 2. 0.6. 3. 0.4. 4. 1,750. 5. 200.

7.7   Discussion Questions: 1. See page 127 of text. 2. See pages 131-132 of text. 3. See pages 133-134 of text. 4. See page 141 of text. 5. See pages 143-144 of text. 6. See pages 145-147 of text.

CHAPTER 8: THE NEO-KEYNESIAN MODEL

Key Concepts

Automatic Stabilizers are those elements of government's policy that reduce fluctuations in aggregate demand in times of booms and recessions.

Real balance or wealth effect refers to the effect of a change in the price level on the purchasing of the amount of money you already have.

Interest rate effect refers to the effect of a change in the price level on the rate of interest.

Consumption effect refers to the effect of a change in the price level on consumer spending.

Investment effect refers to the effect of a change in the price level on business and residential spending on investment or capital goods.

Foreign trade effect refers to the effect of a change in the price level on net exports, i.e. $X - M$.

Chapter Overview

In the Neo-Keynesian model aggregate demand is linked negatively and the aggregate supply positively to the price level. In a depression, expansionary monetary and fiscal policies raise output and employment without causing inflation. In a recession, expansionary monetary and fiscal policies raise output, employment as well as the price level.

If the aggregate supply curve shifts to the left because of a rise in the price of oil or sharply rising wages, output and employment fall and the price level goes up. Stagflation is a state of rising inflation as well as unemployment.

There is a tradeoff between inflation and unemployment, and is known as the Phillips curve. According to the Phillips curve or the creed of deficit financing, which means that State budget deficits are financed primarily by money creation, joblessness can be reduced permanently. Needless to say, such painless and simple way of eradicating unemployment is false.

According to monetarism fluctuations in money supply are the main cause of business fluctuations so that the monetary authority should follow a uniform rule whereby money supply grows at the rate of long run GDP growth, approximating 4 percent.

Rational expectations mean that workers use all available information to form their future expectations. Specifically, expansionary economic policies cause them to believe that inflation is about to rise. The policy of deficit financing followed in the recession of 2001 failed to create expectations of future inflation.

True-False Questions

8.1   Indicate whether the following statements are (T)rue or (F)alse:

_____ 1.   In a booming economy, automatic stabilizers slow the rise in aggregate spending and output and help slow down inflation.

_____ 2.   In the neo-Keynesian model, aggregate demand is not related to the price level.

_____ 3.   A fall in the price level causes consumption spending to increase partly because of lower interest rates and partly because of increased purchasing power.

_____ 4.   The investment effect of a decrease in the price level is unambiguously positive because spending on new homes increases.

_____ 5.   Americans and foreigners tend to buy more American goods and services when the price of American goods and services falls relative to foreign goods and services.

_____ 6.   The aggregate demand curve is very steep because the investment effect is larger than the consumption and foreign trade effects.

_____ 7.   Once the economy reaches full employment, it is impossible to achieve further increases in output or further reductions in the unemployment rate.

_____ 8.   Expansionary fiscal and monetary policies tend to shift the aggregate demand curve to the right.

_____ 9.   Crowding out is unlikely to be an issue when the economy is in a depression because investment spending is already very low.

_____ 10.   The Phillips Curve depicts a negative relationship between the inflation rate and the unemployment rate, but it is unlikely that the position of the Phillips Curve will remain unchanged as inflation escalates.

8.2   **Multiple Choice** – circle the best response:

1.   Which of the following best describes an expansionary, built-in stabilizer?
      a. The increase in income taxes paid when incomes climb in a booming economy.
      b. A decision by Congress to lower income tax rates.
      c. Increased government transfer payments in the form of unemployment compensation during a recession.
      d. A decrease in government support of food stamps and Medicaid.

2.   When the price level declines, the consumption effect causes:
      a. an increase in investment spending resulting from higher interest rates.
      b. an increase in consumption spending resulting from lower interest rates.
      c. an increase in exports and a decrease in imports.
      d. a decrease in consumption spending resulting from reduced purchasing power.

3.   When the price level increases, the foreign trade effect causes:
      a. an increase in both exports and imports.
      b. a decrease in both exports and imports.
      c. an increase in exports and a decrease in imports.
      d. a decrease in exports and an increase in imports.

4.   The investment effect of a price fall is uncertain because:
      a. while households buy fewer new homes, companies buy more machines.
      b. while households buy more new homes, companies buy fewer machines.
      c. households buy fewer new homes and companies buy fewer machines.
      d. households buy more new homes and companies buy more machines.

5.   If the aggregate supply curve is nearly horizontal and the aggregate demand curve shifts to the right, then:
      a. real output will rise substantially with very little effect on the price level.
      b. real output will increase and the price level will increase by the same proportion.
      c. the price level will rise substantially with very little effect on real output.
      d. there will be no effect on either real output or the price level because the aggregate demand curve is very steep.

6. If the aggregate supply curve is nearly vertical and the aggregate demand curve shifts to the right, then:
   a. real output will rise substantially with very little effect on the price level.
   b. real output will increase and the price level will increase by the same proportion.
   c. the price level will rise substantially with very little effect on real output.
   d. there will be no effect on either real output or the price level because the aggregate demand curve is very steep.

7. The phenomenon of crowding out occurs because:
   a. increased government borrowing raises interest rates and investment spending.
   b. increased government borrowing raises interest rates and reduces investment spending.
   c. increased investment spending raises interest rates and forces the government to spend more to service its debt.
   d. investment spending does not depend on the interest rate.

8. Suppose the economy is currently in short-run equilibrium at an output level that is above full employment. What is most likely to happen in the long run?
   a. lower wages cause the short-run aggregate supply curve to shift rightward, causing short-run equilibrium output to fall back to full employment.
   b. higher wages cause the short-run aggregate supply curve to shift rightward, causing short-run equilibrium output to fall back to full employment.
   c. lower wages cause the short-run aggregate supply curve to shift leftward, causing short-run equilibrium output to fall back to full employment.
   d. higher wages cause the short-run aggregate supply curve to shift leftward, causing short-run equilibrium output to fall back to full employment.

9. The major argument of the Monetarist model, pioneered by Milton Friedman, is that:
   a. the monetary sector is the source of most business fluctuations and monetary policy is the most important tool for achieving economic stability.
   b. the investment-goods sector is the source of most business fluctuations and fiscal policy is the most important tool for achieving economic stability.
   c. business fluctuations are unlikely and government should not do anything to promote economic stability.
   d. government policies are ineffective because rational agents always anticipate the consequences of any policy implemented by the government.

10. According to the Rational Expectations model, when workers see repeatedly that government actions raise prices, they react to government's announcement of using a policy of deficit financing by:
   a. increasing the number of labor hours supplied, causing an economic boom.
   b. reducing the number of labor hours supplied, causing a recession.
   c. immediately demanding higher nominal wages to compensate for higher expected inflation.
   d. accepting lower real wages in the short term because they know that eventually both nominal and real wages will rise again.

<u>8.3</u>   **Graphing Questions** – use the graph below to answer the questions.

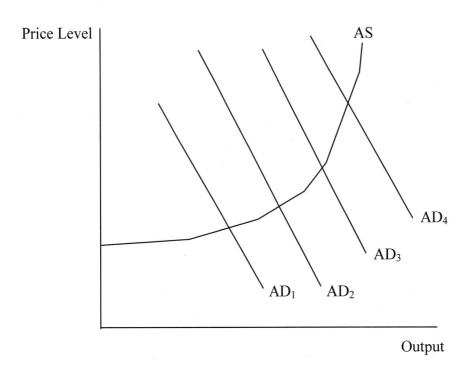

1. If aggregate demand shifts from AD₁ to AD₂ in the graph above, will the resulting change in the price level be relatively small, relatively large, or in between? Will the resulting change in output be relatively small, relatively large, or in between? What will happen to the economy's rate of unemployment as a result of this shift?

2.   If aggregate demand shifts from AD_2 to AD_3 in the graph above, will the resulting change in the price level be relatively small, relatively large, or in between? Will the resulting change in output be relatively small, relatively large, or in between? What will happen to the economy's rate of unemployment as a result of this shift?

3.   If aggregate demand shifts from AD_3 to AD_4 in the graph above, will the resulting change in the price level be relatively small, relatively large, or in between? Will the resulting change in output be relatively small, relatively large, or in between? What will happen to the economy's rate of unemployment as a result of this shift?

8.4   **Graphing Questions** – use the graph below to answer the questions.

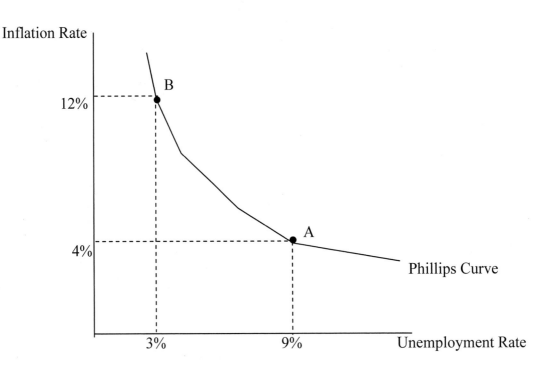

1.   Describe a specific government policy that could cause the economy to move from point A in the graph above to point B. Would this policy likely involve deficit financing?

2.   If the economy's natural rate of unemployment is 5%, can the economy stay at point B in the graph above permanently?

8.5   Discussion Questions

1.   Define and give some examples of automatic stabilizers.

2.   Describe the three effects that come into play when the price level changes, leading to a negatively-sloped aggregate demand curve.

3.   Give examples of expansionary fiscal policy and explain the effect such policies have on aggregate demand. Under what conditions would it be appropriate for the federal government to employ expansionary fiscal policy?

4.   Define and discuss the significance of crowding out.

5.   What was the fundamental flaw with the Phillips Curve according to Milton Friedman? How did Friedman define the "natural" unemployment rate?

6.   Explain why stabilization policies are unlikely to be effective according to the model of Rational Expectations. Do you agree with this conclusion?

The Answer Key

8.1   True/False: 1. T 2. F 3. T 4. F 5. T 6. F 7. F 8. T 9. T 10. T

8.2   Multiple Choice: Find your answers

8.3   Graphing Questions:
1. small; large; unemployment will fall.
2. in between; in between; unemployment will fall.
3. large; small; unemployment will fall.

8.4   Graphing Questions:
1. An expansionary fiscal policy—increase in government spending and/or lower taxes; yes, this would likely involve deficit financing.
2. No, the economy cannot stay at point B permanently—see the flaw of the Phillips Curve on page 175 of the text.

8.5   Discussion Questions: 1. See pages 158-159 of text. 2. See pages 160-161 of text. 3. See pages 167-168 of text. 4. See pages 169-170 of text. 5. See pages 175-176 of text. 6. See pages 177-178 of text.

CHAPTER 9: A CLASSI -KEYNESIAN MODEL

Key Concepts

Capacity Utilization is the fraction of an economy's productive capacity utilized in producing goods and services. It is the highest when the economy is at full employment.

Marginal product of capital is the gain in the economy's output that occurs when one more unit of capital is utilized, keeping other factors of production constant.

The full capacity point occurs in the economy when output cannot rise because of the full utilization of productive capacity. It usually coincides with the point of full employment of labor.

Employment paradox occurs when output falls but employment actually rises.

Chapter Overview

The classi-Keynesian model is a blending of the classical and neo-Keynesian models. The hybrid system retains the assumptions of the classical framework but derives Keynesian conclusions. Thus employment is determined by aggregate demand, while the real and nominal wage spring from the labor-market equilibrium. Nevertheless, Keynesian rigidities can also be accommodated in the new framework.

Even though, thanks to wage-price flexibility, labor supply and labor demand are always equal along the aggregate supply curve, full employment occurs only when the economy operates at the **full capacity** point. This occurs because both employment and the real wage can rise until the full capacity point. A rise in the price level raises **capacity utilization**, whereas a fall in the price level does the opposite.

The real wage is the highest at the full capacity point. Contrast this with various classical and Keynesian systems, where the real wage, contrary to expectations, is the lowest at the point of full employment. Monetary and fiscal expansion generate a rise in capacity utilization, employment, output and the real wage, so long as the economy is in recession, i.e., it is operating below the full capacity point.

Beyond the full capacity point monetary and fiscal expansion cause nothing but inflation. During the two recessions of the 1970s, when the international price of oil soared, output fell but employment rose slightly. This **employment paradox** can be explained only by the classi-Keynesian model, because capacity utilization shrank so much from the rise in energy cost that output fell despite a rise in labor demand, which itself resulted from a sharp rise in the price level.

Important Equations

$$W = P \cdot \text{MPL}$$

and

$$i + \text{energy cost} = P \cdot \text{MPK},$$

where MPK is the marginal product of capital, W is the money wage, P the price level and i the nominal rate of interest. Both factors are combined technologically to generate the output in terms of a production function as

$$Y = F(K, L)$$

and

$$K = \text{CU} \cdot Ko, \ \text{CU} \leq 1,$$

where CU is the fraction representing capacity utilization, and Ko is the fixed stock of capital.

True-False Questions

<u>9.1</u>   Indicate whether the following statements are (T)rue or (F)alse:

_____ 1.   Money is neutral in the classical model, meaning that monetary stimulus cannot cure a recession.

_____ 2.   Neither the Keynesian nor the neo-Keynesian models can explain why involuntary unemployment occurs.

_____ 3.   Economic data indicate that real wages rise during economic upturns and fall during economic downturns.

_____ 4.   The classi-Keynesian model is based on the concept of capacity utilization, which varies across the business cycle.

_____ 5.   In the classi-Keynesian model, an increase in aggregate demand causes an increase in capacity utilization, which leads to an increase in the marginal product of labor and an increase in labor demand.

_____ 6.   When the price level rises, money demand shifts to the right and the nominal interest rate increases while the real interest rate falls.

_____ 7.   Over the past 30 years, the rate of inflation has trended downward while the real interest rate has trended upward.

_____ 8.	In the classi-Keynesian model, full employment occurs when output and employment available from the complete use of all resources are at their highest levels.

_____ 9.	The classi-Keynesian model predicts that an increase in energy prices will cause capacity utilization to fall, which in turn lowers the demand for labor.

_____ 10.	The employment paradox occurs when output falls, capacity utilization declines, but employment rises.

9.2	**Multiple Choice** – circle the best response:

1.	Which of the following is one of the flaws of the classical and neoclassical models?
	a. The models can explain involuntary unemployment with some wage rigidity, but do not explain how the real wage is determined.
	b. The models are unable to explain involuntary unemployment.
	c. The models assume money is not neutral, but there is substantial evidence to the contrary.
	d. All of the above are flaws of the classical and neoclassical models.

2.	Which of the following is one of the flaws of the Keynesian and neo-Keynesian models?
	a. The models can explain involuntary unemployment with some wage rigidity, but do not explain how the real wage is determined.
	b. The models assume money is neutral, but there is substantial evidence to the contrary.
	c. The models predict that the real wage rises in a booming economy and falls in a recessionary economy.
	d. All of the above are flaws of the Keynesian and neo-Keynesian models.

3.	An increase in the price level causes the money demand curve to:
	a. shift rightward and the equilibrium nominal rate of interest to increase.
	b. shift rightward and the equilibrium nominal rate of interest to decrease.
	c. shift leftward and the equilibrium nominal rate of interest to increase.
	d. shift leftward and the equilibrium nominal rate of interest to decrease.

4.   If the money supply function is positively sloped, then an increase in the price level causes the nominal interest rate to:
a. fall and the real interest rate to rise.
b. fall and the real interest rate to fall.
c. rise and the real interest rate to rise.
d. rise and the real interest rate to fall.

5.   If an increase in aggregate demand causes the price level to rise and capacity utilization to increase, then the marginal product of labor _____ and the demand for labor shifts _____.
a. decreases; rightward
b. decreases; leftward
c. increases; rightward
d. increases; leftward

6.   A decrease in the demand for labor causes the equilibrium real wage rate to:
a. increase and the equilibrium level of employment to fall.
b. increase and the equilibrium level of employment to rise.
c. decrease and the equilibrium level of employment to fall.
d. decrease and the equilibrium level of employment to rise.

7.   In the classi-Keynesian model:
a. there is no joblessness.
b. joblessness is always involuntary.
c. joblessness is always voluntary.
d. joblessness is both voluntary and involuntary.

8.   In the classi-Keynesian model:
a. monetary policy is effective until the economy reaches full capacity, then it becomes neutral.
b. monetary policy is always effective.
c. monetary policy is never effective.
d. monetary policy is neutral until the economy reaches full capacity, then it becomes effective.

9. An increase in the price level caused by a leftward shift of aggregate supply causes the demand for labor to:
    a. increase and the accompanying decrease in capacity utilization also increases labor demand.
    b. increase, but the accompanying decrease in capacity utilization reduces labor demand.
    c. decrease, but the accompanying decrease in capacity utilization increases labor demand.
    d. decrease and the accompanying decrease in capacity utilization also reduces labor demand.

10. The employment paradox occurs when:
    a. output falls while employment goes up.
    b. output and employment both fall.
    c. output and employment both rise.
    d. there is no change in either output or employment.

9.3 Graphing Questions

1. Sketch a graph with money demand and money supply and indicate the equilibrium nominal rate of interest in your graph. Now, suppose an increase in aggregate demand causes an increase in the price level. What will happen to money demand and the equilibrium nominal interest rate as a result? Will the change in the nominal interest rate be proportionally as large as the change in the price level?

2. Sketch a graph with labor demand and labor supply and indicate the equilibrium
    real wage rate in your graph. Now, suppose an increase in aggregate demand causes an increase in capacity utilization. What will happen to the marginal product of labor, the labor demand curve, the equilibrium real wage rate, and the equilibrium level of employment as a result? Show these changes in your graph.

3. Sketch a graph with aggregate demand and aggregate supply assuming that
    equilibrium occurs at full capacity. If aggregate demand shifts to the left, what will happen to the price level? What will happen to capacity utilization? What will happen to the marginal product of labor, the demand for labor, the equilibrium real wage rate, and the equilibrium level of employment?

4. Sketch a graph with aggregate demand and aggregate supply assuming that equilibrium occurs at full capacity. If energy prices rise, what will happen to aggregate supply and the price level? What will happen to capacity utilization? Explain how the two effects on labor demand can lead to an employment paradox.

9.4   Discussion Questions

1. Discuss some of the major flaws in the Classical and Neo-Classical frameworks.

2.   Discuss some of the major flaws in the Keynesian and Neo-Keynesian frameworks.

3.   Explain the concept of capacity utilization and how it tends to vary across the business cycle.

4.   Describe the relationship between the rate of inflation, the nominal rate of interest, and the real rate of interest, both theoretically and empirically.

5.   What is the condition for full employment in the classi-Keynesian model? Under what conditions will unemployment prevail in this model?

6.   Explain the employment paradox.

The Answer Key

9.1   True/False: 1. T 2. F 3. T 4. T 5. T 6. T 7. T 8. T 9. T 10. T

9.2   Multiple Choice: 1. B 2. A 3. A 4. D 5. C 6. C 7. D 8. A 9. B 10. A

9.3   Graphing Questions:
1. See graph on page 185 of text; money demand shifts right, the nominal interest rate rises, the price level increases proportionally more than the nominal interest rate.
2. See graph on page 188 of text; the marginal product of labor increases and labor demand shifts right, the equilibrium real wage and level of employment both rise.
3. See graph on page 190 of text; the price level falls and capacity utilization falls, the marginal product of labor falls and labor demand shifts left, the equilibrium real wage and level of employment fall.
4. See graph on page 193 of text; aggregate supply shifts left and the price level increases, capacity utilization falls, there are two effects on labor demand: the higher price level causes labor demand to shift right and the lower capacity utilization causes labor demand to shift left—if the first effect dominates, then there will be an employment paradox (lower output, but higher employment).

9.4   Discussion Questions: 1. See page 181 of text. 2. See page 181 of text. 3. See page 182 of text. 4. See pages 184-187 of text. 5. See pages 188-189 of text. 6. See pages 195-196 of text.

CHAPTER 10 THE ANATOMY OF STOCK MARKET BUBBLES AND CRASHES

Key Concepts

A speculative bubble is born when the law of demand for the purchase of assets such as, stocks, bonds and real estate, breaks down completely. People then buy assets simply because they are expensive and sell them when they are cheaper.

Overinvestment occurs when capital spending grows faster than the nation's output for many years.

A business merger occurs when one company buys another and combines the output and hiring decisions into one unit.

A bubble economy is born when collectively debt, business investment, business mergers and share prices zoom and exceed productivity rise and GDP growth for several years. Speculation thrives, as the public and financial institutions rush to acquire various assets at exorbitant prices.

A stock market crash occurs when share prices fall much faster then the fall in real GDP.

The marginal revenue is the extra revenue that a company receives from the sale of a unit of output.

Key Equations

$$AS = Y = (Y/L)L = AL$$
$$AD = C + I$$
$$C = wL$$
$$\text{Profit} = Y - wL - \text{unsold goods}$$

This last definition only suggests that national profit is equal to sales (output – unsold goods) minus the labor expense. Here Y is output, C is consumption, A is the average product of labor, L is employment, and w is the real wage. We assume that the government budget is initially balanced, and that government spending raises AD and taxes lower AD by equal amounts. We also assume that all wage-income is consumed, and there is no international trade. In equilibrium

$$AS \ = \ AD \ \text{and unsold goods} \ = \ 0$$

or

$$AD \ = \ C + I + \text{new debt} \ = \ AS$$

Under monopolistic competition

$$\text{Money Wage} \ = \ MRPL = MR \bullet MPL$$

where the marginal revenue (MR) is less then the price level. If we divide both sides of the equation by P, we get

$$\text{Real Wage} = \frac{MR}{P} . MPL$$

or

$$\text{Real wage} \ = \ m \bullet MPL$$

In a two-factor economy,

$$Y \ = \ AL \ = \ wL \ + \ \text{profit},$$

or

$$\text{profit} \ = \ AL(1 - w/A)$$

or

$$\frac{profit}{output} \ = \ 1 - \frac{w}{A}$$

Chapter Overview

Share prices rise in proportion to a rise in profits or capital income. Keynesian and neo-classical models are unable to explain why stock market bubbles arise and fall. Normally the stock market moves proportionately with an increase in productivity, because both profits and real wages share equally in the fruit of economic growth. But once in a while, the real wage trails the gains in productivity; then profits (or capital income) and share markets soar; if this process continues for long, stock-market bubbles are born.

A speculative bubble occurs when the law of demand for certain risky assets breaks down. People then buy more of these assets in spite of their soaring prices. On the other side, they buy less of the assets even as their prices fall. The wage gap is defined by the ratio of labor productivity and the real wage; when productivity outpaces real earnings, then the wage gap rises, the labor market becomes distorted, and many unexpected things happen in the economy.

The share market mania or some kind of speculative bubble is born when productivity gains are accompanied by a rise in the wage gap. The increase in the wage gap germinates a rise in the economy's debt, including consumer, corporate and government debt. There were two periods that experienced share-price bubbles in the United States in the 20th century—first in the 1920s and then from 1982 to 2000. Each time the wage gap went up for at least a full decade.

The wage-gap rise also causes overinvestment and a merger mania, both of which, coupled with soaring debt and stock prices, generate a bubble economy. Japan's bubble economy occurred during the 1980s, whereas U.S. bubbles took place in the 1920s and then from 1982 to 2000. Every bubble bursts in the end, because the growing wage gap that creates it also sows the seed of the bubble's destruction, which occurs when debt growth slows down.

U.S. stock market bubbles burst in 1929 and then again from 2000 to 2002. In the aftermath of the bubble occurs a depression or a long period of employment stagnation. The wage gap may rise because of a fall in the minimum real wage, labor-union decline, free trade, rise in regressive taxes such as the Social Security tax and the sales tax, or a persistent decline in market competition.

If the wage gap declines share prices may fall even in high-growth economies, as they did in Germany from 1960 to 1980. Once the bubble economy bursts open, economic policy may be ineffective for a while in curing the stagnation.

True-False Questions

10.1   Indicate whether the following statements are (T)rue or (F)alse:

_____ 1.   When the law of demand for assets breaks down completely, so that their demand is high when price is high and low when price is low, a speculative bubble is born.

_____ 2.   Whenever the real wage grows at the same rate as productivity, a wage gap develops in the economy.

_____ 3.   The two decades of the 1980s and 1990s have much in common with the decade of the 1920s, such as soaring profits, stock prices, consumer debt, and business mergers.

_____ 4.   If real wages grow faster than productivity, then aggregate demand cannot keep pace with aggregate supply without an infusion of debt.

_____ 5.   When the rate of interest is falling, bonds are more attractive than stocks so funds flow into the bond market.

_____ 6.   Since regressive taxation tends to increase labor force participation, it can cause an increase in the wage gap as the increase in labor supply pushes the real wage down proportionally more than the average product of labor.

_____ 7.   Other things the same, if firms have the ability to influence the price of their product, they will produce more and charge a lower price compared to the outcome of perfectly competitive product markets.

_____ 8.   If imports are labor-intensive relative to exports, the result of free trade is an overall decline in domestic demand for labor and an increase in the wage gap.

_____ 9.   If the wage gap declines, stock prices may fall even in high-growth economies—as they did in Germany from 1960 to 1980.

_____ 10.   Traditional supply-side economic policies have proven to be the most effective means of correcting an economic downturn following a stock market collapse.

10.2   **Multiple Choice** – circle the best response:

1.   When the price of a share of Nortel stock was $80, the quantity demanded was very high, but when the price fell to $2 per share, the quantity demanded was very low. This example illustrates:
a. that the law of demand is always valid.
b. a breakdown in the law of demand.
c. that participants in the stock market are always rational.
d. the reason the stock market is efficient.

2.   When the real wage trails labor productivity:
a. the wage gap falls.
b. the wage gap remains constant.
c. the wage gap rises.
d. there is no effect on the wage gap.

3.   Which of the following did <u>not</u> occur during the decade of the 1920s and the decades of the 1980s and 1990s?
a. Macroeconomic policy emphasized industrial and financial deregulation.
b. Government adopted a non-interfering approach to the business sector.
c. Profits, stock prices, and business mergers soared.
d. Consumer debt and government debt both fell.

4. If wages are the main source of demand and productivity the main source of supply, then an increase in the wage gap implies that:
   a. increases in demand will outpace increases in supply, motivating government to use expansionary policies that tend to increase debt.
   b. increases in demand will outpace increases in supply, motivating government to use contractionary policies that tend to reduce debt.
   c. increases in supply will outpace increases in demand, motivating government to use expansionary policies that tend to increase debt.
   d. increases in supply will outpace increases in demand, motivating government to use contractionary policies that tend to reduce debt.

5. If technology causes labor productivity to double and, at the same time, real wages and investment spending double, then:
   a. the wage gap will fall and firms will likely experience inventory depletion.
   b. the wage gap will remain constant and firms will likely experience neither depletion nor accumulation of inventory.
   c. the wage gap will rise and firms will likely experience inventory accumulation.
   d. the wage gap will rise and firms will likely experience neither depletion nor accumulation of inventory.

6. If technology causes labor productivity to double and, at the same time, investment spending doubles but real wages less than double, then:
   a. the wage gap will fall and firms will likely experience inventory depletion unless government uses contractionary policy.
   b. the wage gap will remain constant and firms will likely experience neither depletion nor accumulation of inventory.
   c. the wage gap will rise and firms will likely experience inventory accumulation unless government uses expansionary policy.
   d. the wage gap will rise and firms will likely experience neither depletion nor accumulation of inventory unless government uses expansionary policy.

7. When the wage gap and debt grow:
   a. company profits grow, causing stock prices to rise.
   b. company profits grow, causing stock prices to fall.
   c. company profits fall, causing stock prices to rise.
   d. company profits fall, causing stock prices to fall.

8. A bubble economy is characterized by:
    a. exponential growth in investment, mergers, profits, stock prices, consumer debt, and government debt.
    b. moderate growth in investment, mergers, profits, stock prices, consumer debt, and government debt.
    c. little or not change in investment, mergers, profits, stock prices, consumer debt, and government debt.
    d. sharp declines in investment, mergers, profits, stock prices, consumer debt, and government debt.

9. All of the following are likely explanations for the increase in the wage gap that has occurred since 1970 <u>except</u>:
    a. the declining influence of labor unions.
    b. the erosion of the purchasing power of the minimum wage.
    c. growing reliance on progressive taxation.
    d. growing reliance on free trade.

10. When aggregate supply increases proportionally more than aggregate demand, government policymakers are likely to implement:
    a. expansionary policies to avoid inflation.
    b. expansionary policies to avoid deflation.
    c. contractionary policies to avoid inflation.
    d. contractionary policies to avoid deflation.

10.3 Graphing Questions

1.   Suppose an increase in the labor force participation rate causes the supply of labor to shift to the right. Sketch a graph to illustrate this shift and include the average product of labor (APL) and marginal product of labor (MPL) curves in your graph. Explain what happens to the equilibrium real wage relative to the average product of labor as a result of the increase in labor supply. What does this imply about the wage gap, defined as the ratio of labor productivity to real wage?

2.   **Use the graph below to answer the questions.**

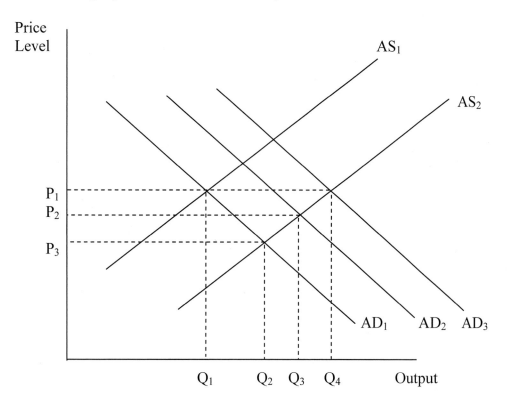

a.   Suppose an improvement in technology causes the aggregate supply curve to shift from AS_1 to AS_2. If the real wage increases in proportion to labor productivity, such that the wage gap is constant, then the aggregate demand curve will shift from AD_1 to AD_3. In this case, describe the economic consequences of the improvement in technology.

b.   Suppose an improvement in technology causes the aggregate supply curve to shift from AS_1 to AS_2. If the real wage increases, but at a slower rate than the increase in labor productivity, such that the wage gap is rising, then the aggregate demand curve will shift from AD_1 to AD_2. In this case, describe the economic consequences of the improvement in technology.

<u>10.4</u>   **Discussion Questions**

1.   Use an example to illustrate a breakdown in the law of demand in asset markets.

2.   Define the wage gap and explain what it means when the wage gap in increasing over time.

3.   Discuss the similarities between the decades of the 1980s and 1990s and the decade of the 1920s.

4.   Explain why an increase in the wage gap and debt cause an increase in company profits. What is the effect of rising profits on stock prices?

5.   Explain how and why a speculative bubble must eventually collapse.

6.   List six explanations for the rising wage gap observed in the U.S. economy since the 1970s.

The Answer Key

10.1   True/False: 1. T 2. F 3. T 4. F 5. F 6. T 7. F 8. T 9. T 10. F

10.2   Multiple choice: Find your answers

10.3   Graphing Questions:
   1. See graph on page 214 of text; the equilibrium real wage will fall; the average product of labor also falls, but not as much; the wage gap rises.
   2. See pages 219-220 of text. In part (a), the wage gap is constant so AD keeps pace with AS and output increases with no change in the price level. In part (b), the wage gap rises and AD does not keep pace with AS, prompting government to take expansionary measure to avoid deflation so debt increases.

10.4   Discussion Questions: 1. See page 199 of text. 2. See page 200 of text. 3. See pages 202-203 of text. 4. See page 208 of text. 5. See pages 212-213 of text. 6. See pages 213-219 of text.

CHAPTER 11: LONG RUN GROWTH AND GROWTH CYCLES

Key Concepts

Demand management policies refer to Keynesian monetary and fiscal policies to maintain an adequate level of aggregate demand, so that the economy is at full employment with restrained inflation.

The business cycle refers to the peaks and valleys that describe the path of real GDP over time. This is mostly a short-run phenomenon.

The growth cycle refers to the peaks and valleys that describe the path of real GDP growth over time. This is also a short-run phenomenon.

The rate of saving is the fraction that a nation saves out of its real GDP.

Returns to scale are constant, if equal rises in capital and labor raise output by the same amount.

Positive externalities refer to the beneficial effects of new technology for the entire society, not just its inventor.

Key Equations

$$Y = AL$$

where Y is output, A is labor productivity, and L is employment. Assuming **full employment**, as in the classical model, the growth in employment equals the growth in labor force. From this relationship, we can write that

$$YG = PG + LG$$

where the "G" around a variable indicates its rate of growth. Thus YG is the rate of growth of output or real GDP, PG is productivity growth or the growth rate in the average product of labor, and LG is the growth rate of labor force. Real business investment minus depreciation of capital defines the **change in capital stock,** i.e.,

$$I - \text{depreciation} = \Delta K$$

For simplicity, we assume that depreciation is zero. Then dividing both sides by K gives us:

$$I/K = \Delta K/K = KG$$

which is the growth rate of capital.

so that

$$\text{Investment} = \text{Savings} = sY,$$

$$KG = \Delta K/K = sY/K$$

where s is the economy-wide saving rate. The growth rate of capital, from this formula, equals the rate of saving times the average product of capital i.e., Y/K. *In equilibrium the growth rate of capital equals the growth rate of labor*, that is,

$$KG = LG = sY/K$$

and output grows at the same rate as either capital or labor provided we assume constant returns to scale.

$$\text{Effective labor growth} = \Delta L/L + \Delta T/T$$

where $\Delta T/T$ is the rate of improvement in technology.

In equilibrium

$$\Delta K/K = \text{Effective labor growth} = \Delta L/L + \Delta T/T$$

In other words, in growth equilibrium capital grows at the same rate as labor and productivity. This, with constant returns to scale, means that output grows at the same rate as labor and productivity, or

$$\Delta Y/Y = \Delta L/L + \Delta T/T$$

or

$$YG = LG + PG$$

Aggregate demand growth may be described as follows:

$$DG = c.CG + v.IG + g.GG - z.TDG$$

where the addition of "G" to a variable indicates its rate of growth, i.e., $DG = \Delta AD/AD$ is the rate of growth in aggregate demand; CG is the growth rate of consumption, with c being its weight or share in GDP; IG is the rate of growth of investment, with v being its weight in GDP, GG is the growth rate of government spending, with g being its weight in GDP, and TDG is the growth in the trade deficit, with z being its weight in GDP. However, supply growth is the same as output growth or YG. Thus

$$SG = PG + EG,$$

In growth equilibrium

$$\text{Demand Growth} = \text{Supply Growth}$$

Chapter Overview

According to Professor Solow's model, a country's rate of GDP growth depends positively on its rate of saving and technological progress that springs from some unknown source. Per-capita GDP growth equals labor productivity growth, and high population growth reduces the standard of living. New growth theory says technological progress depends on choices people and firms make about education, and spending on research and development.

According to new growth theory, associated with Professor Romer, investment in new technology may be more important to economic growth than investment in physical capital, because new ideas and inventions may have positive spillover effects that move from one industry to another.

Both the Solow model and the Romer model slight the demand side of the economy. The Solow-Romer model is unable to explain the growth cycles that now occur every year. A growth cycle describes the fluctuations that occur quarterly or annually in the rate of GDP growth. Such fluctuations can be properly explained only by a theory that gives prominence to both demand and supply growth.

Recent growth fluctuations in the United States have been caused mostly by variations in government spending and the trade deficit. Expansionary monetary and fiscal policy is desirable if growth is too low to provide employment to all job seekers. If growth is too low to absorb all job seekers into the economy, then a **growth recession** occurs.

True-False Questions

11.1   Indicate whether the following statements are (T)rue or (F)alse:

_____ 1.   Recent data on quarterly growth rates for the U.S. economy show almost no variation over time when projected at annual rates.

_____ 2.   If output is growing faster than the population, then per-capita output is increasing.

_____ 3.   If the population of a country is increasing by 4 percent each year, then the

_____ 4.   population can be expected to double in about 70 years.
    If per-capita output is increasing by 2 percent each year, then living standards will approximately double in about 35 years.

_____ 5.   A 10 percent increase in all inputs causes a 10 percent increase in output in an economy with increasing returns to scale.

_____ 6.   Solow's growth theory predicts that nations will have a high per-capita GDP if they have a high savings rate, a high rate of technological advance, and a low rate of population growth.

_____ 7.   Romer's new growth theory is based on the notion that the choices people make in pursuit of profits and the choices nations make in pursuit of growth determine a country's long-term growth trends.

_____ 8.   Technological advances may have positive externalities in the sense that they benefit all, not just their inventor.

_____ 9.   Recent growth fluctuations in the U.S. have been caused by changes in the savings rate and the rate of population growth, not by variations in government spending and the trade deficit.

_____ 10.   If growth is too low to absorb all job seekers in the economy, then a growth recession occurs.

11.2   **Multiple Choice** – circle the best response:

1.   If output is growing at the rate of 4 percent while the labor force is growing at the rate of 1.75 percent, then we can conclude that labor productivity is:
a. growing at the rate of 2.25 percent.
b. growing at the rate of 5.75 percent.
c. falling at the rate of 2.25 percent.
d. falling at the rate of 5.75 percent.

2.   If output is growing at the rate of 4 percent while the labor force is growing at the rate of 1.75 percent, then we can conclude that per-capita output is:
a. growing at the rate of 2.25 percent.
b. growing at the rate of 5.75 percent.
c. falling at the rate of 2.25 percent.
d. falling at the rate of 5.75 percent.

3. According to the rule of 70, if output is growing at the rate of 3.5 percent per year, then output will:
    a. never double.
    b. double in 20 years.
    c. double in 70 years.
    d. double in 245 years.

4. The Solow growth model reaches the conclusion that a country's growth rate:
    a. is constant, regardless of saving behavior or technological progress.
    b. depends negatively on its rate of saving and positively on technology.
    c. depends positively on its rate of saving and technology.
    d. depends negatively on its rate of saving and technology.

5. The Solow growth model predicts that, other things the same, a nation will experience more rapid economic growth as a result of:
    a. a high savings rate.
    b. a high rate of technological advance.
    c. a low rate of population growth.
    d. all of the above contribute to more rapid economic growth in the model.

6. The new growth theory, pioneered by Paul Romer:
    a. fails to explain the source of technical improvements.
    b. fails to explain how technology is linked to economic growth.
    c. explains technical improvements as the product of choices people make.
    d. explains technical improvements as exogenous variables in the model.

7. In an inflationary economy, consumption growth tends to:
    a. rise due to an increase in the purchasing power of money balances and a lower nominal interest rate.
    b. fall due to an increase in the purchasing power of money balances and a lower nominal interest rate.
    c. fall due to a decrease in the purchasing power of money balances and a higher nominal interest rate.
    d. rise due to a decrease in the purchasing power of money balances and a higher nominal interest rate.

8. Assume the economy is initially in equilibrium with a positive inflation rate and a positive GDP growth rate. If demand growth expands and there is no change in supply growth, then, in the new growth equilibrium, there will be:
a. a higher inflation rate and a higher GDP growth rate.
b. a higher inflation rate and a lower GDP growth rate.
c. a lower inflation rate and a higher GDP growth rate.
d. a lower inflation rate and a lower GDP growth rate.

9. Assume the economy is initially in equilibrium with a positive inflation rate and a positive GDP growth rate. If supply growth expands and there is no change in demand growth, then, in the new growth equilibrium, there will be:
a. a higher inflation rate and a higher GDP growth rate.
b. a higher inflation rate and a lower GDP growth rate.
c. a lower inflation rate and a higher GDP growth rate.
d. a lower inflation rate and a lower GDP growth rate.

10. A growth recession occurs when:
a. new jobs are created and the rate of unemployment falls.
b. new jobs are created but the rate of unemployment rises.
c. no new jobs are being created but the rate of unemployment falls.
d. no new jobs are being created and the rate of unemployment rises.

11.3 Graphing Questions

1. Sketch a graph with a Supply Growth curve (positively sloped) and a Demand Growth curve (negatively sloped) assuming equilibrium occurs with positive inflation but negative GDP growth.

2. Sketch a graph with a Supply Growth curve (positively sloped) and a Demand Growth curve (negatively sloped) assuming equilibrium occurs with negative inflation but positive GDP growth.

3. Sketch a graph with a Supply Growth curve (positively sloped) and a Demand Growth curve (negatively sloped) assuming initial equilibrium occurs with positive inflation and positive GDP growth. Graphically illustrate and explain the effect of an increase in demand growth, assuming no change in supply growth.

4. Sketch a graph with a Supply Growth curve (positively sloped) and a Demand Growth curve (negatively sloped) assuming initial equilibrium occurs with positive inflation and positive GDP growth. Graphically illustrate and explain the effect of an increase in supply growth, assuming no change in demand growth.

11.4 Discussion Questions

1. What are the sources of economic growth in the Solow growth model?

2. The Solow growth model explains economic growth as a result of technological progress, among other things. Does the model explain what determines the rate of technological progress?

3. What does the neoclassical growth model predict will happen to real wages and the real return to capital as a result of productivity growth?

4.   Explain why a falling inflation rate would stimulate consumption growth, have little or no effect on investment growth, and stimulate net export growth.

5.   Discuss two reasons why accelerating inflation raises the effective growth of the capital stock and hence productivity growth.

6.   Is there any role for economic policy in minimizing growth fluctuations?

The Answer Key

11.1   True/False: 1. F 2. T 3. F 4. T 5. F 6. T 7. T 8. T 9. F 10. T

11.2   Find your answers

11.3   Graphing Questions:

1. See the graphs on page 247 of text (here, SG and DG intersect in the northwest quadrant).
2. See the graphs on page 247 of text (here, SG and DG intersect in the southeast quadrant).
3. See the graph on page 248 of text.
4. See the graph on page 249 of text.

11.4   Discussion Questions: 1. See pages 236-240 of text. 2. See page 240 of text. 3. See page 242 of text. 4. See pages 244-245 of text. 5. See page 246 of text. 6. See page 251 of text.

CHAPTER 12: INEQUALITY, REGRESSIVE TAXATION AND THE GROWTH SLOWDOWN

Key Concepts

Equity-efficiency trade-off refers to the view that rising inequality increases a country's efficiency, because it generates high savings, which can be turned into higher business investment and capital stock to stimulate output growth.

A progressive tax is one where the rich pay a larger percentage of their income in taxes than the poor.

A regressive tax is one where the poor pay a larger percentage of their income in taxes than the rich.

Ethical economic policy is one that raises the living standard of all, especially the poor.

Unethical economic policy is one that raises the living standard of the few at the expense of the living standard of the masses.

Tax-and-spend policies occur when the government keeps raising taxes to finance its ever-growing spending.

Borrow-and-spend policies occur when the government keeps borrowing money to finace its ever-increasing spending.

Chapter Overview

Income and wealth inequality in the United States is now near the worst it has ever been, virtually back to the levels last experienced prior to the Great Depression. According to Keynes rising inequality lowers the economy's marginal propensity to consume, raises the level of saving, and generates a lower level of output and employment. Some economists think that high inequality is good for society because it increases savings and hence investment, which raises GDP growth.

U.S. history reveals that the highest growth rates after WWII occurred when the top-bracket income tax rate averaged more than 80 percent, as in the 1950s and the 1960s. The poor and the middle class paid very little in the form of Social Security and sales taxes. Thus the tax system was **ultra-progressive.**

Real minimum wage was the highest at the end of the 1960s, just when the unemployment rate was among the lowest at 3.5 percent. Thus, the view that minimum-wage legislation curtails the number of jobs is not supported by history. In fact, a rising minimum wage spurs growth and employment.

The tax system became regressive when the income tax rate began to fall and the Social-Security and sales tax rates started to rise after 1970. After 1980, the tax system became **ultra-regressive**, as the income tax continued to fall, and the Social Security and sales taxes kept rising.

A progressive tax structure leads to a high level of aggregate demand and GDP growth, whereas a regressive system creates low AD and GDP growth. This explains why the 1980s and the 1990s, the decades with the ultra-regressive tax system, generated the worst growth performance in peace-time American history, with the exception of the Great Depression.

History flatly contradicts supply-side economics, which is the reason why economic growth since 1981 has been mediocre. The tax system since 1975 has also become increasingly regressive in other countries, with predictable results. Not surprisingly, their growth record has varied from poor to mediocre. Low growth in Europe, Japan and Canada has resulted in higher rates of unemployment. Ethics and productive efficiency go together. One cannot thrive without the other.

True-False Questions

12.1   Indicate whether the following statements are (T)rue or (F)alse:

_____   1.   The inequality in household income and in individual earnings is far greater today than at any time since the late 1960s.

_____   2.   Keynes believed that a progressive income tax structure was on of the main causes behind the Great Depression.

_____   3.   If the tax rate, as a percentage of income, increases as income increases, then the tax is progressive.

_____   4.   U.S. history shows that when the tax system is highly progressive, economic growth and real wages soar.

_____   5.   Supply-side economists argue that imposing a greater tax burden on the rich harms incentives to save and invest, thus reducing the economy's potential for long-term growth.

_____   6.   During the 1980s, tax cuts led to soaring government budget deficits, which in turn caused U.S. interest rates to reach all-time lows.

_____   7.   High interest rates tend to discourage consumer spending, especially on durable goods such as cars, appliances, and furniture.

_____ 8.   During the 1980s and 1990s, tax breaks were directed primarily at small businesses, causing large corporations to stagnate.

_____ 9.   Historical data convincingly demonstrates that higher minimum wages cause higher rates of unemployment.

_____ 10.   The tax system since 1975 has become increasingly regressive in other countries and their growth rates have suffered as a result.

12.2   **Multiple Choice** – circle the best response:

1.   Between 1980 and 2000, the annual income of the top fifth of U.S. families:
      a. remained roughly constant.
      b. rose about 30 percent.
      c. fell about 20 percent.
      d. fluctuated up and down, but overall did not change over this time period.

2.   Currently, approximately _____ percent of total income goes to the richest 20 percent of households, while approximately _____ percent of total income goes to the poorest 20 percent of households.
      a. 35.4; 2.4
      b. 43.6; 9.4
      c. 49.7; 3.6
      d. 59.1; 5.6

3.   Keynes believed that rising income inequality contributed to the Great Depression because income concentration in a few hands tends to:
      a. raise the marginal propensity to save and aggregate savings.
      b. lower the marginal propensity to save and aggregate savings.
      c. raise the marginal propensity to save and lower aggregate savings.
      d. lower the marginal propensity to save and raise aggregate savings.

4.   The growth argument for inequality, which is based on the notion of an equity-efficiency tradeoff, is based on the belief that:
      a. reduced income inequality leads to higher levels of saving and investment.
      b. when saving increases in excess of investment, aggregate demand falls.
      c. greater income inequality leads to higher levels of saving and investment.
      d. income inequality has no effect on aggregate demand.

5. Which of the following is currently a progressive tax?
    a. the sales tax levied on the purchase and sale of many commodities
    b. the payroll tax paid by employers and employees to fund Social Security
    c. the income tax
    d. all of the above are highly progressive

6. In the post-world war II era, the highest income tax rates prevailed in the:
    a. 1950s and average GDP growth during the decade was relatively high.
    b. 1950s and average GDP growth during this decade was relatively low.
    c. 1980s and average GDP growth during the decade was relatively high.
    d. 1980s and average GDP growth during the decade was relatively low.

7. According to the text, the three culprits for the growth stagnation during the 1980s included all of the following *except*:
    a. the sharp decline in the top-bracket income tax rates.
    b. a sharp reduction in corporate income tax rates.
    c. increases in the social security tax and sales taxes, both of which are regressive.
    d. the dramatic increase in the price of oil.

8. When income inequality rises, the demand growth curve shifts:
    a. rightward, causing GDP growth to rise and inflation to fall.
    b. rightward, causing GDP growth and inflation to rise.
    c. leftward, causing GDP growth to fall and inflation to rise.
    d. leftward, causing GDP growth and inflation to fall.

9. Higher government budget deficits lead to _____ interest rates and _____ aggregate demand, other things the same.
    a. higher; stronger
    b. higher; weaker
    c. lower; stronger
    d. lower; weaker

10. Between 1968 and 2003, the minimum wage:
    a. rose in nominal terms but fell in real terms.
    b. fell in nominal terms but rose in real terms.
    c. rose in both nominal and real terms.
    d. fell in both nominal and real terms.

12.3 Discussion Questions

1. Keynes suggested that rising income inequality was one of the main causes behind the Great Depression. Explain the argument he used.

2. Explain the general relationship between tax rates and economic growth, as demonstrated by U.S. historical data.

3. According to the text, what were the three culprits for the growth stagnation during the 1980s?

4.   Why does progressive taxation improve economic performance and regressive taxation worsen it?

5.   What is the likely effect of large government budgetary deficits on interest rates? How does this likely change in interest rates affect the economy?

6.   What has happened to the minimum wage, in real terms, since 1968? How has this change apparently affected unemployment? How has this change affected aggregate demand?

The Answer Key

12.1   True/False: 1. T 2. F 3. T 4. T 5. T 6. F 7. T 8. F 9. F 10. T

12.2   Find your answers

12.3   Discussion Questions: 1. See page 255 of text. 2. See pages 256-258 of text. 3. See page 259 of text. 4. See page 261 of text. 5. See page 265 of text. 6. See pages 266-267 of text.

CHAPTER 13: THE SUPPLY OF MONEY

Key Concepts

Money is anything that is commonly accepted as a medium of exchange.

A store of value is something that can be used to preserve wealth over time.

Liquidity of an asset is a quality that refers to the ease with which goods and services can be converted into money.

A unit of account is something in which numerical variables can be expressed.

Fiat money is one that is decreed by the government.

Bank Reserves (BR) are cash or assets quickly convertible into cash in the hands of commercial banks and savings and loan associations.

The reserve requirement ratio (rrr) is the fraction of their demand deposits (DDs) that banks must keep in reserve to meet the daily cash needs of their customers.

Money multiplier is the multiple by which banks can turn their cash into creation of money.

Discount rate is the interest rate that the federal reserve system (i.e. the Fed) charges commercial banks for lending them money.

Federal funds rate is the interest rate that banks charge each other for loans.

Open market operations refer to the Fed's purchase or sale of federal government's bonds in the open market.

Key Formulas

$$M1 = \text{Cash in the hands of the public} + \text{checking accounts} + \text{traveler's checks}$$

$$M2 = M1 + \text{savings accounts} + \text{small CDs} + \text{money market mutual funds}$$

$$M1 = \text{Public's Cash Holding} + DDs = \text{Public's Cash} + \frac{BR}{rrr}$$

$$\text{Money multiplier} = 1/rrr$$

where DDs are demand deposits or checking accounts.

Chapter Overview

Money is anything that serves as a medium of exchange, store of value and unit of account. Two definitions of money supply are widely used in the world—M1 and M2. M1 includes cash in the hands of the public, checking accounts or demand deposits, and traveler's checks. M2 includes M1, savings deposits, small CDs that are less than $100,000, and money market mutual funds.

The very definition of M1 indicates that banks are heavily involved in the creation of money. In a 100 percent reserve system, money supply equals cash in public hands plus that held in bank vaults. In a fractional reserve system, banks lend their excess reserves and open demand deposits in the name of the borrowers. This way, banks create money.

The reserve requirement ratio (*rrr*) is a legal requirement that the Fed imposes on banking institutions, which currently have to set about 10 percent of their demand deposits in reserve to meet the public's needs for spending. The Fed, consisting of 12 regional banks, is the nickname of the Federal Reserve System, which was established in 1914. The Fed acts as the nation's central bank.

The Fed can regulate the supply of money in three ways—by changing the reserve requirement ratio, the discount rate, and the federal funds rate. The federal funds rate changes when the Fed buys or sells federal bonds openly in the bond market—a practice called open market operations.

The discount rate is the interest rate that the Fed charges for making loans to banks, whereas the federal funds rate is the interest fee that banks charge each other for loans. Even if the Fed succeeds in controlling money growth, the policy objective of the Fed may be thwarted if the Fed chairperson adopts faulty policies. The cycle of money growth shows that the Fed has no control over money supply in the long run. Alan Greenspan had a major role in creating the bubble economy in the 1990s, and the subsequent share-market crash.

True-False Questions

13.1   Indicate whether the following statements are (T)rue or (F)alse:

_____   1.   Money is anything that is commonly accepted as a medium of exchange.

_____   2.   Money is anything that serves as a store of value.

_____ 3. The M1 definition of the money supply includes only cash in the hands of the public because only cash is considered to be perfectly liquid.

_____ 4. Based on the total amount of paper currency in circulation in 2002, it would seem that a large number of U.S. dollars are circulating abroad.

_____ 5. A system in which banks make loans and keep only a fraction of their deposits in reserve is called fractional-reserve banking.

_____ 6. Under fractional-reserve banking, banks have the power to create money.

_____ 7. If a bank's cash reserves equal $1,000,000 and the bank is holding a 20 percent reserve ratio, then the bank has total demand deposits equal to $200,000.

_____ 8. The volume of banking lending varies inversely with the reserve ratio held by banks.

_____ 9. Congress passed the Federal Reserve Act in 1913 in response to a severe banking panic that occurred in 1907.

_____ 10. The Fed sets legal reserve requirements to ensure that banks have enough cash on hand to satisfy everyone in the event that all depositors decide to withdraw their account balances.

True-False Questions

13.2 Indicate whether the following statements are (T)rue or (F)alse:

_____ 1. If banks can lend all they want, keeping bank reserves equal to the minimum required, then demand deposits will equal bank reserves multiplied by the money multiplier.

_____ 2. The simple money multiplier is equal to the required reserve ratio.

_____ 3. If the public decides to reduce cash holdings and bank reserves increase, then it is likely that M1 will increase due to banking lending activity.

_____ 4. The Board of Governors of the Federal Reserve System consists of 12 members, one from each district of the Federal Reserve.

_____ 5. Alan Greenspan is the current chair of the Board of Governors of the Federal Reserve System.

_____ 6. The members of the Board of Governors of the Federal Reserve System also serve on the Federal Open Market Committee (FOMC).

_____ 7. The Fed's most frequently used tool for bringing about a desired change in the money supply is to raise or lower the required reserve ratio.

_____ 8. Changes in the discount rate serve as a signaling device more than as an actual instrument for bringing about a desired change in the money supply.

_____ 9. The Fed typically buys bonds in the open market in order to raise bank reserves and bring about an increase in the money supply.

_____ 10. In the Keynesian model, monetary policy impacts the economy by first altering the rate of interest in bond and money markets, and then affecting the components of aggregate demand.

13.3 **Multiple Choice** – circle the best response:

1. Which of the following is *not* one of the functions of money?
   a. medium of exchange
   b. unit of account
   c. inflation hedge
   d. store of value

2. When a shopkeeper states the price of a good in dollars, she is using money as a:
   a. store of value.
   b. unit of account.
   c. medium of exchange.
   d. standard of liquidity.

3. The M2 definition of the money supply includes:
   a. M1 plus some other assets such as savings accounts.
   b. assets such as savings accounts, but does not include M1.
   c. only perfectly liquid assets.
   d. bank deposits of all kinds, but not cash.

4.   Fractional-reserve banking is viable because, on any given day:
a. cash withdrawals exceed cash deposits.
b. no one ever withdraws cash.
c. banks have enough cash to match all deposits.
d. depositors need only a small portion of their funds to make transactions.

5.   When a bank makes a $1,000 loan to a bank customer:
a. the money supply goes up by $1,000.
b. the money supply is not affected.
c. the money supply goes up by a fraction of $1,000.
d. there is no way to predict what might happen to the money supply as a result.

6.   If the required reserve ratio is 10 percent, then a bank that receives a $10,000 deposit can:
a. immediately make a loan equal to $100,000.
b. immediately make a loan equal to $900,000.
c. lend $10,000, but the new money will likely add reserves to another bank.
d. lend $9,000, but the new money will likely add reserves to another bank.

7.   If the banking system has reserves equal to $120 billion and the required reserve ratio is 12.5 percent, then a reasonable estimate for total demand deposits is:
a. $15 billion.
b. $120 billion.
c. $960 billion.
d. $1,200 billion.

8.   If the banking system has reserves equal to $250 billion and the required reserve ratio is 10 percent, then a reasonable estimate for total demand deposits is:
a. $25 billion.
b. $250 billion.
c. $2,500 billion.
d. $25,000 billion.

9.   If the required reserve ratio is 12.5 percent, then the simple money multiplier is:
a. 5.
b. 8.
c. 10.
d. 12.

10. If the required reserve ratio is 10 percent, then the simple money multiplier is:
    a. 5.
    b. 8.
    c. 10.
    d. 12.

13.4 **Multiple Choice** – circle the best response:

1. The Federal Reserve System:
   a. was established in 1913 in reaction to banking panics.
   b. provides deposit insurance on accounts up to $100,000.
   c. serves as the central bank for the entire world.
   d. all of the above are true

2. When the Fed lowers the required reserve ratio:
   a. banks have less lending capacity so the money supply is likely to contract.
   b. banks have greater lending capacity so the money supply is likely to expand.
   c. the money multiplier falls.
   d. the money supply and the money multiplier remain unchanged.

3. Members of the Federal Reserve Board of Governors are:
   a. elected by the general population to serve lifetime terms.
   b. selected from the Senate to serve rotating terms.
   c. appointed by the President to serve fixed, non-renewable terms.
   d. appointed by the Senate to serve unlimited terms.

4. When banks borrow funds from the Fed, they must pay an interest fee, referred to as the:
   a. prime rate.
   b. federal funds rate.
   c. discount rate.
   d. bond rate.

5. When a bank borrows funds from another bank, it must pay an interest fee, referred to as the:
   a. prime rate.
   b. federal funds rate.
   c. discount rate.
   d. bond rate.

6. To avoid a shortage of money, or a credit crunch, the Fed would most likely:
   a. buy bonds in the open market.
   b. sell bonds in the open market.
   c. raise both the discount rate and the federal funds rate.
   d. raise the required reserve ratio.

7. According to Monetarists, if velocity is constant and output is growing at the rate of 3.5 percent per year due to technological improvements and productivity gains, then the Fed should:
   a. hold the money supply constant to maintain price stability.
   b. allow the money supply to grow at 3.5 percent per year to maintain price stability.
   c. allow the money supply to grow faster than 3.5 percent per year to foster a higher rate of economic growth.
   d. wait and see what happens to the inflation rate before deciding on a monetary growth rate.

8. If the Fed is buying bonds in the open market, then the money supply will:
   a. increase, causing the equilibrium interest rate to increase.
   b. increase, causing the equilibrium interest rate to decrease.
   c. decrease, causing the equilibrium interest rate to increase.
   d. decrease, causing the equilibrium interest rate to decrease.

9. If the demand for bonds increases, then bond prices will:
   a. fall and bond yields will rise.
   b. fall and bond yields will fall.
   c. rise and bond yields will rise.
   d. rise and bond yields will fall.

10. The phrase "irrational exuberance" was coined by:
    a. Alan Greenspan to describe the booming stock market in the 1990s.
    b. George Bush to describe the booming stock market in the 1990s.
    c. Paul Volcker to describe the stock market crash in 1987.
    d. Alan Greenspan to describe the stock market crash in 1987.

13.5   **Problems**

1.   Suppose that the public's holding of cash equals $80, M1 equals $480, and bank reserves, which are $40, are exactly equal to the minimum amount required. Calculate the values for demand deposits and the required reserve ratio based on this data.

2.   What happens to the money multiplier if the required reserve ratio is reduced from 12.5 percent to 10 percent?

3.   Suppose that the money supply is initially equal to $520, with $260 worth of currency in circulation and $260 worth of demand deposits. If the monetary base is $312, how much are bank reserves? What percentage of demand deposits are banks holding on reserve?

13.6   Graphing Questions

1.   Sketch a graph depicting money demand and money supply and indicate the initial equilibrium rate of interest in your graph. Illustrate the effect of an increase in the money supply on the equilibrium rate of interest.

2.   Sketch a graph depicting bond demand and bond supply and indicate the initial equilibrium bond price in your graph. Illustrate the effect of an increase in bond demand on the equilibrium bond price.

13.7 **Discussion Questions**

1.   List and discuss the functions of money.

2.   Explain the differences between the M1, M2, and M3 definitions of the money supply.

3.   Approximately how much U.S. paper currency is in circulation? Given the adult population of the U.S., estimate how much cash each person has on hand, assuming all cash can be accounted for this way. Does is seem reasonable that people keep this much cash? What other explanations can you offer for the "missing money"?

4.   Explain the significance of fractional-reserve banking.

5.   Use a pyramid diagram to outline the basic structure of the Federal Reserve System. Describe the membership of the Board of Governors and the Federal Open Market Committee.

6.   List and briefly describe each of the tools used by the Federal Reserve to control the U.S. money supply.

The Answer Key

13.1　True/False:　1. T　2. T　3. F　4. T　5. T　6. T　7. F　8. T　9. T　10. F

13.2　Find your answers

13.3　Multiple Choice:　1. C　2. B　3. A　4. D　5. A　6. D　7. C　8. C　9. B　10. C

13.4　Find your answers

13.5　Problems:
　　　1. Demand Deposits = $400 and the required reserve ratio = 10 percent.
　　　2. The money multiplier increases from 8 to 10.
　　　3. Bank Reserves = $52 and the reserve ratio = 20 percent.

13.6　Graphing Questions:　1. See the money market graph on page 287 of text.　2. See the bond market graph on page 287 of text.

13.7　Discussion Questions:　1. See pages 271-272 of text.　2. See pages 272-273 of text.　3. See pages 273-274 of text.　4. See pages 275-276 of text.　5. See pages 280-281 of text.　6. See pages 281-286 of text.

CHAPTER 14: AN OPEN ECONOMY

Key Concepts

A closed economy is one that has little or no reliance on foreign trade. Its trade to GDP ratio is no higher than 10 percent.

An open economy is one that relies heavily on foreign trade; its trade to GDP ratio significantly exceeds 10 percent.

A natural importer is one that cannot prosper without foreign trade. The United States, Japan, Canada, China and Saudi Arabia are natural importers.

A production possibilities curve (PPC) is a curve representing all efficient and feasible points of production in an economy divided into two main sectors.

The consumption gain from trade is the increase in the consumption of at least one good without a decrease in the consumption of any other.

The production gain from trade is the increase in real GDP caused by international trade.

The Growth gain from trade is the rise in GDP growth arising from the import of cheaper capital goods.

The rate of exchange is the foreign currency value of a nation's domestic currency.

G-7 countries is a group of nations including the United States, Canada, Japan, the United Kingdom, France, Italy and Germany. The G-7 has now become **G-8** after admitting Russia.

The interest rate paradox occurs when the trade deficit rises and the rate of interest falls.

The foreign trade multiplier is the effect of a change in autonomous spending on real GDP in an open economy.

Key Formulas

$$R = \text{no. of euros/dollar}$$

where R is the euro-dollar exchange rate.

National demand or American aggregate expenditure (AE) equals:

$$AE = C + I + G,$$

whereas in equilibrium

$$AD = C + I + G + X - M = AS$$

Therefore

$$TD = M - X = C + I + G - AS$$
$$= AE - AS$$

Thus the trade deficit (TD) is the difference between aggregate expenditure and aggregate supply or GDP.

$$P = P^*/R = P^*\$/euros.$$

$$P = \frac{P^*(1+t)}{R}$$

where P is the domestic price level, P^* is the price level in the rest of the world, and t is the rate of tariff on imports.

$$GDP = A^*/(mps + mpi)$$

where A^* is autonomous spending, mps is the marginal propensity to save, and mpi is the marginal propensity to import.

Chapter Overview

Through much of its history, the United States was practically a closed economy, as both imports and exports were miniscule relative to GDP. The GDP share of each hovered around 5 percent, so that trade as a percentage of GDP was close to 10 percent. Since 1970 the nation has become an open economy, and seen its GDP share of total trade rise slowly but steadily. Today this share exceeds 25 percent. This is a remarkable transformation for the country in barely three decades, with momentous consequences.

Countries open up their economies because they obtain a variety of gains from trade, including a consumption gain, a production gain and possibly a growth gain. The consumption gain arises from a rise in the availability of goods from a constant level of output. The production gain arises from the availability of cheaper raw materials from abroad. Finally the growth gain stems from access to inexpensive imports of capital goods.

The United States reaps yet another gain, because the dollar is a key currency, which is widely used for transactions throughout the world. There are some other key currencies as well—the euro, the yen, the pound, the Swiss franc—but the dollar is the most sought-after.

For about two decades, America has amassed a business empire, which confers certain privileges to the nation that only imperialist countries enjoyed in the past. The colonial masters used to collect taxes and free gifts from their colonies. The United States has no colonies, but since 1983 a portion of its imports has essentially come free, because the world is content to exchange its surplus goods for paper dollars, which cost practically nothing to produce.

Most nations have to offer high interest rates to attract foreign funds and finance their trade deficit, but its business empire enables the United States to avoid this discomfort. In fact, foreign countries, in their self interest, park their dollar hoard back into American financial assets to keep their currencies undervalued and to enjoy the fruit of their trade surpluses.

The rising trade deficit caused the U.S. interest rate to fall in the 1990s. This is the interest rate paradox. The Trade deficit normally reduces a country's aggregate demand, but in the United States it raised aggregate demand during the 1990s. The reason was the falling rate of interest that stimulated a housing boom and a high-tech investment boom.

After the stock market crash in 2001 the trade deficit began to have a negative impact on U.S growth and employment, as the interest rate plunged because of the Fed's ultra-expansionary monetary policy, thereby neutralizing the positive impact of the trade shortfall.

The rate of exchange is the relative price between any two currencies. The dollar rate may be defined as the units of a foreign currency needed to buy one dollar. This way the foreign exchange value of the dollar can be explored in terms of the usual forces of demand and supply.

The recent stock market crash caused a fall in the global demand for the dollar, generating its depreciation in world markets. Normally currency depreciation eliminates a country's trade shortfall, at least after a while. But such has not been the case with the American deficit since 1983. The dollar has waxed and waned, but the deficit is forever.

The open economy multiplier is smaller than the closed economy multiplier, because imports add another leakage to the spending stream. The foreign trade multiplier creates economic interdependence in the world, so that growth in one major area spreads across the globe. The open economy multiplier reduces the effectiveness of economic policy.

True-False Questions

14.1   Indicate whether the following statements are (T)rue or (F)alse:

_____   1.   Since 1970 the U.S. has become an open economy, experiencing a
slow and steady increase in both imports and exports.

_____ 2.   Free trade can potentially lead to consumption gains, but production and economic growth always decline as a nation participates more heavily in international trade.

_____ 3.   When a nation imports raw materials, production costs tend to fall and aggregate supply shifts rightward.

_____ 4.   Free trade spurs productive efficiency because cheaper imported capital raises the growth of the country's capital stock and embodies new technology.

_____ 5.   The distribution of income is always more equal in a free trade equilibrium than it is in an equilibrium with no international trade.

_____ 6.   A rising trade deficit always causes a nation's interest rate to rise.

_____ 7.   If the value of the dollar changed from 90 yen to 80 yen, then it would be correct to say that the dollar appreciated against the yen.

_____ 8.   The recent stock market crash caused a fall in the global demand for the dollar, generating its depreciation in world markets.

_____ 9.   Depreciation of the U.S. dollar in world markets during the past decade has reduced imports into the U.S. and increased exports from the U.S.

_____ 10.   In general, the open economy multiplier is smaller than the closed economy multiplier, so economic policy is less effective in an open economy.

14.2   **Multiple Choice** – circle the best response:

Use the graph below to answer questions 1 – 3.

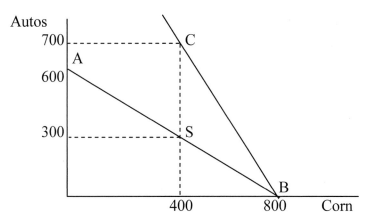

1.   If this nation's production possibilities curve is given by the line AB, then, in the absence of free trade, the relative price of one unit of corn is:
a. 1/2
b. 3/4
c. 1 1/3
d. 2

2.   If this nation moves from an initial equilibrium at point S to a new free trade equilibrium at point C, then the consumption gains from trade are equal to:
a. 100 autos.
b. 300 autos.
c. 400 autos.
d. 700 autos.

3.   Assuming the relative price of corn in world markets is given by the slope of the line BC, this country would benefit from free trade by producing at point:
a. A
b. B
c. C
d. S

4.   The gains from free trade are likely to include all of the following *except* a:
a. consumption gain.
b. production gain.
c. more equal distribution of income.
d. growth gain.

5.	Free trade may have a negative effect on aggregate demand if it causes:
	a. a worsening of the distribution of income.
	b. an increase in the capital stock.
	c. a decrease in the price of imported capital goods.
	d. a decrease in the price of imported consumption goods.

6.	Which of the following is not considered one of the world's "key currencies"?
	a. the dollar
	b. the rial
	c. the euro
	d. the yen

7.	Bond prices are:
	a. not related to market interest rates.
	b. directly related to market interest rates.
	c. inversely related to market interest rates.
	d. constant because once purchased, a bond cannot be resold.

8.	The "interest rate paradox" occurs when a nation experiences:
	a. lower interest rates along with trade deficits.
	b. higher interest rates along with trade deficits.
	c. a balance of trade, in spite of relatively low interest rates.
	d. a balance of trade, in spite of relatively high interest rates.

9.	A larger trade deficit may have a positive effect on aggregate demand if it leads to:
	a. lower interest rates, which encourages a higher rate of saving.
	b. higher interest rates, which can increase consumer durables and housing investment.
	c. higher interest rates, which encourages a higher rate of saving.
	d. lower interest rates, which can increase housing investment and the purchase of consumer durables.

10.	If the marginal propensity to save (mps) is 0.2 and the marginal propensity to import (mpi) is 0.05, then the closed economy multiplier is equal to _____ and the open economy multiplier is equal to _____.
	a. 4; 5
	b. 5; 4
	c. 10; 5
	d. 5; 10

14.3 Graphing Questions

1. Suppose a nation imports less expensive machines that embody improved technology. How would this affect the nation's supply growth (SG)? Illustrate this change in the graph below and indicate its effect on the rate of inflation and GDP growth.

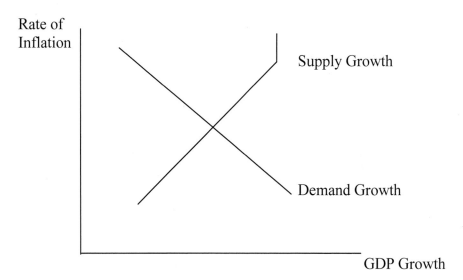

2. Describe three events that would likely increase the global demand for dollars. Graphically illustrate the effect of an increase in the demand for dollars. As a result of this shift, would the dollar appreciate or depreciate?

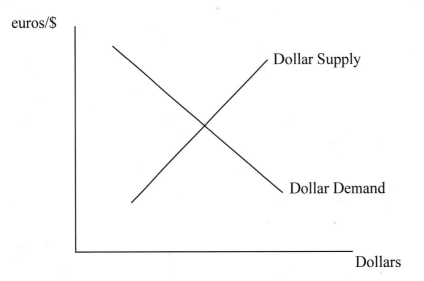

euros/$

Dollar Supply

Dollar Demand

Dollars

14.4   **Discussion Questions**

1.   Discuss the similarities between a business empire and a colonial empire.

2.   Previously-issued bonds are traded in the secondary market. Explain the relationship between bond prices and yields in this market.

3.   Explain the interest rate paradox.

4.   Discuss the hypothesis of "twin deficits".

5.   For America, trade deficits have had two effects—one positive and the other

negative. Explain these two effects.

6.   Does economic policy tend to be more or less effective in an open economy compared to a closed economy? Explain.

The Answer Key

14.1   True/False: 1. T   2. F   3. T   4. T   5. F   6. F   7. F   8. T   9. F   10. T

14.2   Find your answers

14.3   Graphing Questions:
1. See the graph on page 300 of text.
2. See the graph on page 311 of text (change the decrease in the demand for dollars to an increase). An increase in the demand for dollars could come about due to higher U.S. exports, more tourists in the U.S., or more foreign investors willing to park their funds in American financial institutions. An increase in the demand for dollars would cause the dollar to appreciate against the euro.

14.4   Discussion Questions:
1. See pages 301-302 of text.
2. See page 307 of text.
3. See page 309 of text.
4. See pages 312-313 of text.
5. See page 315 of text.
6. See page 317 of text.

CHAPTER 15: THE REAL WAGE AND EXECUTIVE COMPENSATION

Key Concepts

Automation refers to the effect of new labor-saving technology that reduces the demand for labor.

New-process technology is the discovery of new cost-saving ways to produce the same products.

New-product technology is the discovery of new goods and services that satisfy human needs.

Skill-biased technical change refers mainly to the discovery of computers that reduced the demand for unskilled workers and increased the demand for skilled workers.

Chapter Overview

The behavior of real wages in the United States is now one of the most contentious issues in economics. Contrary to what you would expect in a growing economy, real earnings of a vast majority of the workforce have not only become exceedingly unequal among a variety of workers but have also suffered a nearly relentless decline since the early 1970s. It was fashionable in the 1980s to argue that declining productivity growth was the culprit for the wage stagnation. But productivity never declined, only it rose at a slower pace. This is then an explanation for the slowdown in wage growth, not for the outright fall in the real wage.

A popular explanation today is that skill-biased technical change has raised the real wage of the skilled worker at the expense of the unskilled worker. This type of technological progress, however, is the same thing as automation, which has occurred all through American industrial revolution, without ever reducing the real wage of any worker until 1972. So the technology explanation is not consistent with facts of history. Even during the Great Depression, real wages of those employed went up.

Regressive taxation, wherein the tax burden rises for the poor and the middle class, causes a fall in aggregate demand, capacity utilization and hence in the demand for labor. It also leads to a rise in labor supply. All this partly explains why the average real wage stagnated amidst improving technology and rising national productivity after 1972.

Growing trade since 1970 is another reason why automation has caused a fall in the real wage of unskilled workers. In the past, new products produced on American soil used to absorb unskilled labor released through the process of increased automation. But with tariffs gone, American firms have been busy relocating their plants abroad, especially in subsistence-wage countries. Automation now lowers the demand for unskilled work, with no offsetting increase coming from new-product technologies, which now materialize in foreign countries.

Declining business competition has increased the power of the CEOs and the boards of directors, enabling them to set salaries for each other. CEOs now sit on the boards of many companies, and in effect set compensation for themselves. The main source of the outrageous pay of the CEOs and some company directors is the relocation of factories to low-wage nations. This sharply lowers the cost of production and raises company profits, of which a part goes to the CEOs, another part goes to CEO-friendly directors and the rest is declared to shareholders. This way globalization has helped reduce the real wage of the unskilled worker, while enriching the CEOs and some directors beyond imagination.

True-False Questions

15.1   Indicate whether the following statements are (T)rue or (F)alse:

_____   1.   Real wages of production workers in the U.S. have generally fallen since 1972, despite rising productivity.

_____   2.   During the 1950s and 1960s, average wages in the U.S. grew rapidly, and the dispersion around this growing average changed very little.

_____   3.   Skill-biased technical change causes the average wage of both skilled and unskilled workers to fall.

_____   4.   When labor demand shifts to the left, the equilibrium wage rate and level of employment falls.

_____   5.   Regressive taxation contributes to wage stagnation in spite of improving national productivity from advancing technology.

_____   6.   A fall in labor demand accompanied by an increase in labor supply results in little or no change in the equilibrium real wage.

_____   7.   A fall in labor demand accompanied by an increase in labor supply results in little or no change in the equilibrium level of employment.

_____   8.   When imports are labor-intensive relative to exports, trade expansion leads to wage losses because of falling labor demand.

_____   9.   New-process technology tends to reduce the demand for unskilled work, while new-product technology tends to raise the demand for unskilled work.

_____ 10.   There have been no events in recent U.S. history that explain the trends of falling wages and rising productivity.

15.2   **Multiple Choice** – circle the best response:

1.   With skill-biased technical change, the demand for unskilled labor:
       a. decreases, causing the wages of unskilled workers to fall.
       b. decreases, causing the wages of unskilled workers to rise.
       c. increases, causing the wages of unskilled workers to fall.
       d. increases, causing the wages of unskilled workers to rise.

2.   With skill-biased technical change, the demand for skilled labor:
       a. decreases, causing the wages of skilled workers to fall.
       b. decreases, causing the wages of skilled workers to rise.
       c. increases, causing the wages of skilled workers to fall.
       d. increases, causing the wages of skilled workers to rise.

3.   Economic researchers have found that the real wage of skilled workers has:
       a. risen in recent years, while the real wage of unskilled workers has fallen.
       b. fallen in recent years, while the real wage of unskilled workers has risen.
       c. risen in recent years, along with the real wage of unskilled workers.
       d. fallen in recent years, along with the real wage of unskilled workers.

4.   All of the following are new phenomena that have occurred since the early 1970s
       except:
       a. U.S. dependence on foreign oil.
       b. growing international trade and a persistent trade deficit.
       c. less regressive taxation and falling income inequality.
       d. large federal budget deficits and a growing national debt.

5.   Regressive taxation tends to reduce the demand for labor because it:
       a. lowers the aggregate demand for goods and raises the rate of capacity
          utilization.
       b. lowers the aggregate demand for goods, and the rate of capacity utilization.
       c. raises the aggregate demand for goods and lowers the rate of capacity
          utilization.
       d. raises the aggregate demand for goods, then the rate of capacity utilization.

6. An increase in labor supply combined with a decrease in labor demand results in:
    a. a decrease in the equilibrium wage with little or no change in employment.
    b. an increase in the equilibrium wage with little or no change in employment.
    c. a decrease in employment with little or no change in the equilibrium wage.
    d. an increase in employment with little or no change in the equilibrium wage.

7. New-process technology tends to:
    a. reduce the demand for unskilled work because new products can absorb those laid off from the introduction of new-process technologies.
    b. raise the demand for unskilled work because new products can absorb those laid off from the introduction of new-process technologies.
    c. reduce the demand for unskilled work because the same output can be produced with fewer low-skilled workers.
    d. raise the demand for unskilled work because the same output can be produced with fewer low-skilled workers.

8. New-product technology tends to:
    a. reduce the demand for unskilled work because new products can absorb those laid off from the introduction of new-process technologies.
    b. raise the demand for unskilled work because new products can absorb those laid off from the introduction of new-process technologies.
    c. reduce the demand for unskilled work because the same output can be produced with fewer low-skilled workers.
    d. raise the demand for unskilled work because the same output can be produced with fewer low-skilled workers.

9. When a firm faces a downward-sloping demand curve:
    a. marginal revenue is equal to average revenue.
    b. marginal revenue is greater than average revenue.
    c. marginal revenue is less than average revenue.
    d. the firm maximizes profit by setting price equal to marginal cost.

10. A monopolistically competitive firm maximizes profit by producing where:
    a. marginal revenue equals marginal cost, and the firm sets price equal to marginal cost.
    b. price equals marginal cost.
    c. price equals marginal revenue.
    d. marginal revenue equals marginal cost, but the firm sets price above marginal cost.

15.3 Graphing Questions

Use the graph for a monopolistically competitive firm to answer the questions below.

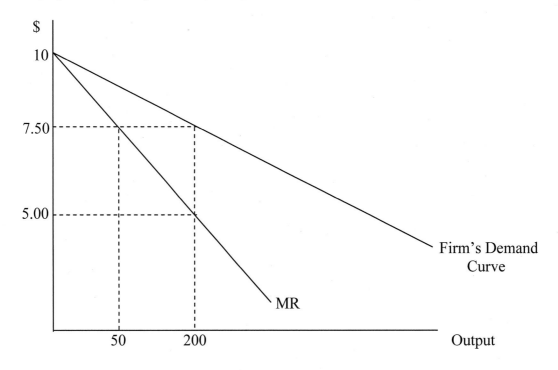

1. If marginal cost (MC) is constant and equal to $5.00, how much output will a profit-maximizing firm produce? What price will the firm charge for each unit of output?

2.   Calculate the firm's total revenue using the values for price and output calculated above. If the firm's total costs are equal to $1,000, how much profit does it earn?

3.   What would happen to this firm's output, price, and profit if the marginal cost fell?

The Answer Key

15.1   True/False: 1. T   2. T   3. F   4. T   5. T   6. F   7. T   8. T   9. T   10. F

15.2   Find your answers

15.3   Graphing Questions:
1.   Output = 200 and price = $7.50.
2.   Total Revenue = $1,500 and Profit = $500.
3. The price would fall, output would rise, and profit would increase.